CLXX

The Vision and the Need

by the same author

BEACONSFIELD AND BOLINGBROKE

Mr. Rudyard Kipling takes a bloomin' day aht, on the blasted 'eath, along with Britannia, 'is gurl.

THE VISION
AND THE NEED

*Late Victorian
Imperialist Aims*

by

RICHARD FABER

FABER AND FABER

24 Russell Square

London

First published in mcmlxvi
by Faber and Faber Limited
24 Russell Square London WC1
Printed in Great Britain by
Latimer Trend & Co Ltd Plymouth

Contents

*

The frontispiece is reproduced from
The Poets Corner by Max Beerbohm
by kind permission of William Heinemann

'Came the Whisper, came the Vision,
        came the Power with the Need,
Till the soul that is not man's soul
        was lent to us to lead.'

from Kipling's
A Song of the English

Introduction

In the space of a generation, the British Empire has disintegrated, or been transformed, in a way that is extraordinary even in retrospect. 'How marvellous it all is . . .' said Rosebery at Glasgow two generations ago. Marvellous in its growth; almost equally marvellous in its dissolution. Yet the Empire seldom made, in either phase, the impact on the mother country that its friends or enemies would have wished. This is among the many odd features of its story. We know that we have witnessed, during our lifetime, a very unusual historical process; but few of us feel it with a close personal sense of shock, relief or even surprise.

Yet few British families have not, at some stage, been closely affected by the existence of the Empire. My own family must resemble a good many, with its quota of Victorian ancestors who took part in imperial wars, emigrated to 'the colonies' or helped to govern India. My mother spent a part of her childhood in India and my father was at one time intended by his parents for the Indian Civil Service. With many others I served in the Indian Ocean, obscurely, towards the end of the last war, when Burma and Malaya were recovered from the Japanese. Since then my work has taken me to the Middle East and to Africa, where I have seen British and French colonies or protectorates before and after independence. I only give this as a fairly typical example. Other lives and families have of course been much more deeply involved in imperial happenings.

One might have thought that such frequent and complex ties could not be cut, or altered, and leave so little obvious trace in British life. Yet, by and large, we seem to have outlived our

Empire with surprisingly little embarrassment or emotion, other than an uneasy feeling that we have a new role to find, that we need some new politicial cries at home and some new clothes for international wear. If there is nostalgia today for the red-coloured maps of thirty years ago (when the amount of red was still deeply gratifying to a child at school), it is oddly unobtrusive.

People are usually more indifferent to public events than the historian is apt to assume; in any case, modern life calls for quick adaptability. Nevertheless, the relative painlessness of this withering away tends to confirm that the British imperial purpose was normally peripheral rather than central, that it really was—in a sense—'absent-minded'. If of course one regards independence as having been the rightful aim of our Empire, our reaction to its loss should perhaps be not only painless but proud. But this would be to simplify the reasons for which the Empire was in fact won, held and lost—and I wonder whether a strong sense of complacency is any more usual than one of regret.

The change would no doubt have been felt still less if it were not for the one period in our history when a majority—or at least an important minority—of the British people seem to have been powerfully attached in peacetime to an imperial vocation. The Imperialist sentiment of the 'nineties, however short-lived its heyday and however limited its effect on affairs, has cast its shadows up till our own time. Perhaps we are only now reaching a point where we can analyse this mood without partisan feeling. We are still near enough to it to understand some of the passions it aroused, but we are far enough off to view it with fair detachment. It will be a long time before any kind of definitive judgment can be passed on the British imperial achievement; but perhaps we can begin to put into perspective some of the motives behind it.

This book is primarily concerned with ideas rather than events. Its object is to analyse, situate and compare the aims of leading British Imperialists towards the turn of the century. When I first embarked on it, I think I expected to find some peculiarly expansive quality in the late Victorian mood, which could be parallelled in other empire-building periods. I hoped it would be possible to discover something about this mood that would help to explain why certain peoples, at certain moments in history, have been driven to conquer and expand. As I studied the subject, however, I realized that this was a misleading way of approaching it: British Imperialism in the late nineteenth century was a complicated phenomenon, containing elements of withdrawal as well as of expansion. The atmosphere of 'glad, confident, morning' was a good deal less pervasive than I had imagined.

My original notion led me to make a particular study of Kipling's Imperialism, since his writings seemed likely to throw the fullest light on the mood I wanted to explore. This explains the rather disproportionate detail in which I have treated them. I hope this detail can still be justified, in spite of the way in which the emphasis of the book has shifted. For one thing, so far as I know, Kipling's Imperialist ideas have not been described so exclusively before— though many insights into them have of course been given by his critics and apologists. For another, Kipling is the only writer of genius who devoted himself seriously to the Imperialist movement in Great Britain. He was, of course, an artist or a preacher, rather than an economist or a philosopher; he was in no sense the Bentham or Cobden of the Imperialist School. His works did not offer a reasoned justification of Empire: they evoked its austere mysteries through portrayal and emotional effect. Nevertheless, the portrait was carefully studied and the emotional effect powerful. Kipling may have had little direct influence on affairs (perhaps Seeley did more to shape the views of responsible statesmen); but his writings coloured the attitude of great numbers of his countrymen. The strength of his influence, which continued even after he had become unfashionable, is reflected in the violent reaction it provoked.

A list of works which I have found useful in preparing this book is given at the end—more by way of acknowledgment than as a 'guide to further reading'. (Even for that purpose it is incomplete; one cannot treat a subject of this sort without drawing on a wide range of sources, sometimes unconsciously.) It will be obvious how much I owe to some of these works, particularly in the treatment of the historical background. My chief debts are, I hope, mentioned in the text. Otherwise I have only supplied references where they seemed important to the argument and could not be guessed from the context.

I am conscious of many shortcomings and can only plead the usual difficulties of preparing and writing a book at different times and in different places and in moments of leisure from ordinary work. Kipling has, as usual, a suitably bracing message:

Man must finish off his work—
Right or wrong, his daily work—
And without excuses.

I

The Background

Empires have been won and held for many reasons. It would be far beyond the scope of this book to attempt a survey of the different forms that imperialism has taken in ancient and in modern times, or of the various motives that have inspired imperialists of different periods and races. But even a superficial analysis soon reveals a few basic themes. I shall be referring later to six motives for imperial expansion, which seem fundamental:

(*a*) *The Colonizing Motive:* the need to provide space for surplus, or dissident, or—in the case of convict settlements—criminal, population.

'Imperialism' of this sort should, of course, more correctly be called 'colonization'. But colonization has often involved the subjection of native peoples—a properly 'imperial' task—and colonies have usually passed through a phase of attachment to metropolitan empires.

(*b*) *The Economic Motive:* at its more primitive a lust for loot or tribute; in a developed form a search for markets or materials; at its most sophisticated this motive implies economic or commercial development supposed to be mutually beneficial.

(*c*) *The Aggressive Motive:* desire for revenge, excitement, power or prestige, whether for the fun of it or to impress others. The simple urge to trample on weak but refractory peoples, or to advertise power and strength, seems to have influenced some imperialist monarchs, for instance the Assyrians, in the past. This motive has not been lacking in modern times, though it has come to play a subordinate role except when refined into forms such as the following:

Empire-building for the sake of 'keeping up with the Joneses': the belief that the acquisition or maintenance of an Empire is, or might become, necessary to enjoy Great Power prestige.

Fin-de-siècle theories, based on 'the survival of the fittest', that the race will be to the fleet and the fight to the strong; that nature is fierce and bloody and that peoples must either come out on top or go under.

(*d*) *The Strategic Motive:* the acquisition of territory in order to safeguard the mother country and its lines of communication, or to protect other dependencies acquired for other motives.

(*e*) *The Missionary Motive:* the ambition to proselytize; to convert other peoples to a religion, a culture or a way of life.

(*f*) *The Leadership Motive:* the conviction of superior ability to provide orderly government, whether as a permanent proprietor or as a temporary trustee.

Almost any combination of these six motives is conceivable, though the first may involve the evacuation or extermination of native peoples and to that extent not be compatible with the two last. The original cause of imperial advance may not, of course, be the same as the reasons given later to justify it—either because it does not look good enough, or because another object has in fact intervened. The two last motives, when sincere, may be thought altruistic. The others make no pretence to be so; though refined forms of the 'Economic Motive' can have an element of altruism and strategic bases are sometimes presented as sources of local wealth. Because of their apparently altruistic character the 'Missionary' and 'Leadership' motives are most likely to be invoked by civilized peoples who feel the need to justify their expansion. But the more selfish motives can also provide respectable material for apology: the 'Strategic Motive' on the grounds of self-defence; the 'Economic' and even the 'Aggressive'motives when the life-blood, or international standing, of the imperial nation seem to be at stake. Where there is empty land colonization barely seems to need justifying; if it involves the subjection of native races an additional, less selfish, motive may be pleaded on its behalf; native extermination—seldom deliberately planned by any central authority—has more often been ignored than defended[1].

The basic motives of empire-builders are perhaps simpler to analyse than the great variety of methods they have used. But one important distinction of method is easily noted. Some imperial techniques have emphasized the difference between rulers and ruled; others have stressed their potential likeness and sought to increase it. 'Assimilatory' methods of this latter kind may be adopted as the most convenient way of ruling an empire acquired through almost any motive. Even the 'Leadership' type of Imperialist, when acting as a temporary trustee, is likely to encourage a measure of assimilation, if only in administrative procedures. But the 'Assimilatory' method belongs above all to the 'Missionary'[2] Imperialist; indeed, wherever this method is practised and for whatever original reason, Imperialism qualifies for justification on 'Missionary' grounds.

The other technique, which separates rulers from ruled, will be called the 'Exclusive' method here, for want of a better word. It goes naturally with most forms of 'Aggressive' or 'Leadership' Imperialism, but it is necessarily opposed, in the long term, to the aims of the 'Missionary'. 'Economic' or 'Strategic' empires may use either technique, depending on circumstances. 'Exclusion' does not, of course, necessarily involve a contemptuous attitude on the part of the rulers; it can sometimes imply respect for indigenous, as well as for metropolitan, standards.

An imperial power may well practise cultural, but not political,

---

[1] Though some of the early American settlers may almost have been inclined to regard it as a religious duty.
[2] In the sense, not necessarily religious, given on p. 16 above.

assimilation. Or it may practise both cultural and political assimilation, without promoting racial fusion. In fact there have been few cases, at least in modern times, when an imperial power has achieved, or even seriously aimed at, racial assimilation —though the example of the Portuguese in Brazil and of the Arabs in parts of North Africa suggests that, in certain circumstances, it is possible for a conquering minority to assimilate racially a sufficiently substantial part of the conquered people to facilitate cultural or political assimilation.

It is also open to an imperial power to assimilate an advanced or cooperative minority of a subject race, while practising 'Exclusion' towards the rest. Something like this seems to have happened in Portuguese Africa.

Another phenomenon is that of 'assimilation in reverse'. The conqueror can come under the influence of his subjects, either because their civilization is of a higher order (*'Graecia capta ferum victorem cepit . . .'*), or through a sort of *nostalgie de la boue*, or because of sheer unwillingness to make the necessary Imperialist effort ('going native'). Like assimilation, 'assimilation in reverse' can be more or less partial or complete; it can apply to a minority or to a majority. But, if an imperial situation is to exist at all, a process of this kind is likely to start culturally and socially rather than politically. A remarkably complete case of eventual 'assimilation in reverse' seems to have been that of the Moors who invaded the central Sahara in the sixteenth century.

Over the ages there have been numerous empires: empires, both ancient and modern, in the Middle East; empires, since the beginnings of recorded history, in India, China and South-East Asia; the great classical empires of Greece and Rome; barbaric empires in the Dark Ages; the religious empires of Islam and the Papacy; the mercantile empires of Mediterranean ports; the empires of the New World; ephemeral empires in the Sahara; the gradually developing land empire of Russia; the overseas empires of Spain, Portugal, Holland, France, Great Britain, Belgium and Germany.

I think it could be shewn that the origin of all these empires lay in one or more of the motives listed above. Even if a thorough classification suggested somewhat different categories (for instance some sub-division of (*c*)), I believe the outlines would stand. It would take volumes to substantiate this claim; but I shall try to illustrate it briefly from the history of the British Empire since its beginnings. Late Victorian Imperialism grew out of, and reacted against, past imperial attitudes and events; it cannot be understood without some attempt at wider analysis and comparison.

The next few pages offer a preliminary, and very summary, sketch of the principles displayed in the Athenian, Roman and French Empires. Because of the importance of classical studies in the education of the British ruling class during the seventeenth, eighteenth and nineteenth centuries, the example of the classical empires and cultures had a powerful effect on British attitudes towards Empire. Adam Smith found it natural to begin the chapter 'Of Colonies' in *Wealth of Nations* with a comparison between modern colonies and those of Greece and Rome; Macaulay wrote in 1835: 'What the Greek and Latin were to the contemporaries of More and Ascham, our tongue is to the people of India'. The late Victorian Imperialists were heirs to this classical tradition and the same comparisons came readily to their minds. French imperial experience probably had less influence on British (and *vice versa*), though French and British colonial administrators sometimes envied, and may occasionally have learned from, each other. But, at the end of the nineteenth century, France was Britain's chief colleague, or rival, in overseas expansion. Some comparison in space, as well as in time, may throw late Victorian Imperialism into sharper relief.

2. THE ATHENIAN APPROACH

The Athenian Empire lasted for under a century. It originated in a confederacy of Greek islands and cities formed early in the fifth century B.C. to deter Persia (an active, but already declining, imperial power) from attempting a fresh invasion of Hellas. Athens, still wearing the laurels of Marathon and Salamis, was the natural leader of the confederacy by virtue of her energy and resources; in the early days she did not need to resort to force.

Gradually, however, the zeal of the confederates weakened as the Persian danger seemed to recede. The payment of tribute came to be accepted in lieu of military or naval contributions; there were revolts which Athens, becoming a ruler rather than a leader, was obliged to quell; the defender of Greek freedom against foreign imperialism ended up as an imperial power herself. By this time both the security of Athens, exposed to the jealousy and even hatred of the Greek world, and her seaward-looking economy, seemed bound up with the maintenance of her Empire. She continued to perform some services in return for the tribute she exacted; her policing of the seas ensured safety of trade. But in 444 B.C. the Athenian leaders took a symbolic, and bitterly controversial, step by devoting surplus imperial funds (whether war booty or unused tribute) to the construction of temples at the capital, for the relief of local unemployment and the edification of posterity. There was no longer any doubt about the subject status of the tributaries.

The extent of the Empire's organization and the degree of Athenian control are still uncertain. But there was a standard coinage; settlements of Athenians were established at points throughout the Empire; there were instances of Athenian interference on behalf of democratic constitutions.

The Empire collapsed after Sparta's victory in the Peloponnesian war. It had always been opposed, even in Athens, by the landowning conservatives, the *demos* being more alive to its economic advantages. The subjects of the Empire were not barbarians but fellow-Greeks; yet Greek colonial tradition favoured purely sentimental links, without any political dependence, between colonies and their founding cities. This induced a feeling of guilt which Pericles and his supporters—if the speeches in Thucydides are a guide—tried to exorcise on three grounds. First, there was the straightforward argument that it would be dangerous to national security and prosperity to let the Empire go. Second, there was the theme of the glorious civilization made possible by the Empire. In the magnificent Funeral Speech Thucydides makes Pericles urge his hearers (perhaps these were really Periclean words) to become 'lovers' of their city, telling them that their present unpopularity was of small account compared with the brilliance of their achievement and the fame it would leave behind. Third, there was the colder note struck by the Athenian Embassy to Sparta before the war and by the Athenian representatives at Melos: the recognition of a law of nature that the lesser would always fall under the power of the stronger, that the strong were not to be blamed for ruling, but deserved praise if they used their power with moderation.

It looks as if the 'Economic Motive', the 'Strategic Motive,' and the 'Aggressive Motive' (the last in, for Pericles, a highly idealized form) were all at work in the Athenian Empire. (The 'Colonizing Motive' had, of course, played its part before the curtain went up.) Justification of empire by the level of civilization it permits in the imperial state seems, basically, to imply a sophisticated form of the 'Economic Motive'. It can only be urged by imperialists who are so confident of their own glory and virtue as to prefer their claims, quite frankly, to those of their subjects. Not much is to be heard of this particular argument in British imperial theory (trade was regarded as *mutually* beneficial). But India was virtually in the position of a tributary state for a period in the eighteenth century and certainly made a contribution, if a relatively unimportant one, to the level of British domestic civilization at the time.

The Athenian Empire, which was short-lived and had rather unusual characteristics, may not seem to provide much material important to a comparative study of British Imperialism. Nevertheless, as a result of the cultural brilliance of fifth century Athens, of the dramatic genius of Thucydides and of the prevalence of classical studies in eighteenth century and nineteenth century Britain, it has had a certain effect on British imperial thought. In the first place the Athenian Empire flourished under a democratic government; it was the oligarchs who were the 'Little Athenians'. This gave it a certain attraction as a precedent for British liberal imperialists, whose sympathies would be on the Athenian side, as against that of reactionary, unenlightened, Sparta, in the Peloponnesian War. Cromer pointed out that the idea of Imperialism, as later understood, 'was wholly foreign to the Greek mind' and that:

'. . . the undisciplined and idealistic Greek, with his intense individuality, was far less suitable to carry an Imperial policy into execution than the austere and practical Roman.' But he found the Athenian experience relevant to the British; he thought it suggested that, though democracy run riot must be fatal to sane imperial policies, democratic institutions were not necessarily incompatible with them.[1] In the second place, the Athenian Empire, like the British but unlike the Roman, was based on command of the sea. There was also a general similarity between the Greek and British colonial traditions: the tendency—again not found in the Roman Empire—for settlement colonies to develop on independent lines, while retaining a certain piety towards the mother country.

The Athenian example could influence British opponents, as well as partisans, of Empire. Its failure, combined with the usual tendency of Greek colonies towards autonomy, was in the minds of the British 'separatists', such as the historian Grote, who had some effect on public opinion in the decades after the independence of the American colonies. A later generation, hostile to jingo Imperialism at the end of the nineteenth century, drew from Thucydides the lesson that Athens had abandoned morality, overreached her strength and met the inevitable reward of her *hubris*—and that the same fate was in store for Great Britain.

This having been said, it remains true that Rome had a much more positive effect on British imperial theory, particularly at the end of the nineteenth century. The Roman Empire was, after all, an infinitely more important concern than the Athenian; its organization was more thorough, or at least better-known; the public-school Englishman tended to feel more in common with the Roman than the Greek. Furthermore, we had had some experience of Roman Imperialism ourselves.

3. THE ROMAN APPROACH

The most striking feature of the Roman Empire was its success: success in the width of its conquests, in the length of its rule,

[1] *Ancient and Modern Imperialism.*

in the depth of its penetration and in the closeness of its administrative texture. In Victorian times Imperialists may have been more struck by its eventual disintegration; but we can now see that no imperial achievement, in modern times, has been so lasting or complete. The Roman Empire grew gradually and reluctantly in accordance with events rather than design, continually seeking surer and more defensible frontiers. The 'Strategic Motive' seems throughout to have predominated, though other motives (in the case of Britain, an interest in her metals) contributed to the legions' advance.

The Romans were not ashamed of their Empire; the propagandists of the Augustan era were able to write of it, with conviction, as a source of pride. There is a distinctly jingo note in certain passages of Horace and Vergil. Even the freedom-loving Tacitus, so firmly opposed to despotism at home, does not seem to have condemned Rome's expansion abroad. He respects those who resist it, taking it for granted that brave men will fight for their freedom and have a right to detest their conquerors. Thus he puts fighting words in the mouths of rebellious chieftains and writes, in *Agricola*, of the Gauls: '*mox segnitia cum otio intravit, amissa virtute pariter ac libertate.*' But he was a patriot who admired the career of his father-in-law in the imperial service. Although he sympathized with its adversaries his writings convey a sense of Rome's imperial mission; it was in the nature of things that courage would struggle, but also that strength would win.

At any rate there is no direct criticism of imperial pretensions in Tacitus, such as there is of the growing power of the emperors in internal affairs. He writes of the former with a detachment lacking in his treatment of the latter. In *Germania* he can recount the habits of 'savage' tribes with an interest and absence of condescension that would do credit to a modern anthropologist. But he is also ready to justify the Empire. Thus, in the *Histories* (IV 73), Cerialis vindicates the Roman record to the Treviri and Lingonae on the grounds that Rome invaded Gaul at the request of their ancestors (who sought protection against the Germans) and not through greed; that Roman law had superseded continual strife; that Rome only exacted from her subjects in Gaul the means to keep the peace; and that these subjects had their share of the duties and privileges of empire. '. . . *ipsi plerumque legionibus nostris praesidetis, ipsi has aliasque provincias regitis; nihil separatum clausumve.*'

'No separation or exclusion.' This was not invariably true in fact, though more so in Gaul, particularly in what is now the French *Midi*, than further afield. But even in the case of less favoured provinces there is ample evidence of the extent to which Rome's subjects, or their descendants, were able to become her rulers, to rise to the Senate, and eventually to the purple. Bright, no Imperialist, speaking in the House of Commons in 1853, referred to the Romans as great, but also wise, conquerors: 'The nations they conquered were impressed so indelibly with the intellectual characters of their masters, that after fourteen centuries of decadence the traces of civilization are still distinguishable. Why should we not act a similar part in India?'[1] Cromer argued that, except in its early Indian period, the British Empire was much more humane than the Roman and much less rapacious. But he had to admit that no modern imperial nation had 'shewn powers of assimilation at all comparable to those displayed by the Romans.'[2]

There were of course reasons for this success in assimilation, as Cromer pointed out: nationalism was less of an organized force; there was an apparent lack of colour prejudice; religious fanaticism was only really intense among the Jews; language posed less of a problem; the theatre of imperial operations was relatively compact; there was no power capable of playing a rival role. Nor was the success achieved without suppression on a wide, and often savage, scale. But judgment goes, finally, by results; and these were impressive.

Roman *assimilation* had a particularly strong influence on the French imperial tradition. It was Roman *discipline* that caught the imagination of the British Imperialists of the late nineteenth century: the emphasis on law and order; the solid organization of the army; the imperturbability of pro-consuls in the face of popular

[1] Quoted in *Concept of Empire*.
[2] *Ancient and Modern Imperialism*.

clamour. Rhodes apparently liked to be reminded of his facial resemblance to the busts of certain Roman Emperors; 'Remember always that you are a Roman' was a favourite quotation of his.[1] The Roman system of complementing direct administration with Client Kingdoms had points in common with the *régime* of Princely States in India or, more remotely, with the later practice of 'Indirect Rule' in Africa. If the *Pax Britannica* was hailed in Latin it was because the *Pax Romana* served as a model for comparison and inspiration.

Like most great enterprises the progress of the Roman Empire was marked by many faults and crimes. No doubt it suppressed or corrupted interesting, and sometimes admirable, 'native' arts and customs. It caused much human suffering—perhaps still more boredom. We do not know enough about the conditions of life in the different classes and regions of the Empire to accept as proven Gibbon's famous verdict on the Silver Age in the second century A.D.[2] Nevertheless, even if Gibbon's verdict were thought too favourable, it would be difficult not to conclude, at this distance of time, that the Empire was, as far as any system of government can be said to be, a net gain to humanity. It furthered the spread of more developed forms of law and knowledge. It created a sense of European unity, which survived to mitigate the national divisions of later times. It seems probable that, over the long period of its rule, a larger number of people enjoyed peace and prosperity than would otherwise have been the case.

Britain was an outlying territory—won late, abandoned early, and afterwards much disturbed by invasion. It is scarcely possible, now, to judge the effect of the 363 years of her subjection to Rome. We still have Roman roads and place names; but the more important influences are the less identifiable. Whether or not such influences can still be traced, there is at least no question of what we owe to Rome, less directly, through Catholicism and the Renaissance. In spite of occasional tendencies to

[1] Lockhart and Woodhouse: p. 31.
[2] 'If a man were called to fix the period in the history of the world, during which the condition of the human race was most happy and prosperous, he would, without hesitation, name that which elapsed from the death of Domitian to the accession of Commodus.'

romanticize Boadicea and Caractacus (Kipling would presumably have described our Celtic ancestors as 'fluttered', 'wild' and 'sullen') most Englishmen who consider the problem at all are more likely to feel proud of their Roman past than ashamed of it.

Even those who do not take this view will not be surprised to find it colouring, for good or ill, the outlook of the British Imperialists.

4. THE FRENCH APPROACH

Like other empire-builders the French were driven by various motives. They colonized little, compared with the British; when they did so, it was for reasons of policy rather than because of population pressure. Between the years of 1871 to 1911, at the time when they created their extensive African Empire, there was in fact a decline of population in France. However, important French colonies had already taken root in Canada and Algeria.

The 'Economic Motive' was always powerful. The economy of the first French Empire had been based on Colbert's mercantilism, which set an enduring pattern, Pressure from business houses contributed, as it did with the British, to expansion in West Africa. Desire for markets and for capital outlets was perhaps the chief motive behind the revival of French Imperialism in the last two decades of the nineteenth century. (It is significant that, despite industrialization, the value of French exports had diminished from 4,518 million francs in 1876 to 4,281 millions in 1886.[1])

The rulers of France have seldom discounted prestige. Thirst for military glory influenced the Algerian expedition and the imperial exploits of the Second Empire. Competition with other powers, particularly Great Britain, played an essential part throughout the eighteenth century and during the 'Scramble for Africa'. On the other hand the 'Strategic Motive' counted for less with continental France than with maritime Britain, except during the struggles between the two countries.

---

[1] *The History of French Colonial Policy 1870–1925* by S. H. Roberts: p. 18.

The 'Missionary Motive' may usually have been a secondary one; but it was scarcely ever absent. Roman Catholics and revolutionaries were alike persuaded of France's *mission civilisatrice*. The Frenchman, who has been described as 'an inveterate proselytizer',[1] has good reason to know the value of his culture and its power to attract others.

The 'Leadership Motive' seems, on the whole, to have been less prevalent, though Frenchmen have sometimes claimed that their relative lack of colour prejudice, combined with their relatively successful attempts to penetrate 'native' psychology' made them better fitted than others to give sympathetic guidance to Asiatic and African peoples.

This is not the place to outline the history of the French Empire. French Imperialists of the seventeenth and eighteenth centuries had had grand designs; but Canada and India were lost to the British; Louisiana was sold by Napoleon to the U.S.A.; by 1880 the only important French dependencies were Algeria, Senegal, New Caledonia, Cochin-China, the French West Indies and the Island of Reunion. The subsequent extension of French rule to South-East Asia and in North, West and Equatorial Africa was part of a process which began in the early 'eighties, during the brief years when Jules Ferry was in power. Tunisia was occupied in 1881. In the following five years Annan and Tonkin were brought under a protectorate and the French took possession of Madagascar. There was also expansion, of a less dramatic kind, in West and Equatorial Africa.

Ferry had to face a good deal of opposition and was often obliged to be secretive about the Government's colonial ambitions. By and large overseas expansion seems to have been unpopular in the France of the 'eighties, because it was held to weaken the country, to waste men and money, to involve an alliance with the German ex-enemy and to distract attention from the basic question of recovering Alsace-Lorraine. There was no wave of popular enthusiasm really comparable to the gusts of Imperialist sentiment in late nineteenth century Britain. Among the informed public there seems to have been little

---

[1] Roberts: *op. cit.:* p. 94

support for colonial expansion before 1881 ;[1] it was by no means whole-hearted even after that date. However, there was a gradual growth of interest, one of the first signs being the hero's welcome given to Brazza on his return to France from Equatorial Africa in June, 1882. A corpus of officials, soldiers and businessmen took shape, who were directly concerned—for patriotic or selfish reasons—in maintaining, or enlarging, the Empire. By 1892 there were ninety-one deputies, drawn from all parts of the Chamber, ready to form a colonially-minded group.

A corollary of the relative lack of public interest in the Empire was that the conduct of imperial policy in France tended to be a more professional and esoteric affair than in Great Britain. Colonial government was carried on with more centralized control from Paris, but under less parliamentary supervision.

Ferry's chief motive seems to have been economic. In 1885 he described colonial policy as 'the daughter of industrial policy.' He thought it urgent, particularly in view of the rising tariffs of other countries (Germany and the U.S.A.), to create colonial markets for metropolitan industry and colonial outlets for metropolitan capital. He said in the Chamber on July 28, 1885 : *'Les colonies sont pour les pays riches un placement de capitaux des plus avantageux . . .'* and : *'Dans la crise que traversent toutes les industries européennes la fondation d'une colonie, c'est la création d'un débouché. . . .'*

There were also other motives. The French naval authorities no doubt urged the need for coaling stations around the world. Ferry was certainly conscious of the prestige factor : he told the Chamber in 1884 : *'Rayonner sans agir . . . croyez-le bien, c'est abdiquer et . . . c'est descendre du premier rang au troisième ou au quatrième.'* He was also a proselytist, urging that France had a duty to civilize what he called, rather loftily, *'les nations barbares'.* This argument seems to have been well received in the Chamber, though the extreme left were apt to protest about the Rights of Man. Neither Ferry nor, with rare exceptions, his opponents,[2]

[1] Cf. *Prelude to the Partition of West Africa* by J. D. Hargreaves: p. 200.
[2] Cf. *Jules Ferry et le Partage du Monde* by F. Pisani-Ferry: p. 40.

regarded the independence of less civilized peoples as a serious obstacle to his projects.

There were no doubt other, less prominent, Frenchmen who shared and helped to form Ferry's ambition to extend French rule overseas, however little their views were reflected in contemporary politics and journalism. Ferry himself was apparently influenced by a book by the economist, Leroy-Beaulieu, which appeared in 1874 under the title: *De la Colonisation chez les Peuples Modernes*.[1] Its title-page bears a quotation from John Stuart Mill, about the value of colonies as outlets for capital. Ferry cited this passage in a parliamentary speech in 1885, in justification of his policy.

De la Colonisation chez les Peuples Modernes is a sober work, solidly argued and dryly prosaic. It begins with a comparative survey of colonization in modern times; deals with French colonial failures and prospects with resigned melancholy and tempered hope; considers whether it is economically profitable for a country to have colonies and concludes that, on the whole, it is; distinguishes the different types of colonies and the ways of making them prosperous; ends, finally, with a purple passage or two, in which the economist allows himself a more romantic glimpse of his subject:

'*La colonisation est la force expansive d'un peuple, c'est sa puissance de réproduction, c'est sa dilatation et sa multiplication à travers les espaces; c'est la soumission de l'univers ou d'une vaste partie à sa langue, à ses moeurs, à ses idées et à ses lois . . . le peuple qui colonise le plus est le premier peuple; s'il ne l'est pas aujourd'hui, il il sera demain.*'[2]

Apart from these passages, the book, like Seeley's *Expansion of England*, is remarkably free from the exalted nationalism that one might expect to find in a work regarded as an Imperialist gospel. Writing in the Free-Trade spirit of the Second Empire, Leroy- Beaulieu maintains that there is no need for the mother-country to insist on exclusive commercial links with her colonies

---

[1] Cf. p. 89 for the influence of this book abroad.
[2] *Op. Cit.:* pp. 605 and 606.

(*'le pacte colonial'*). He argues that the natural ties of language, race, education and manners are the best, and indeed the only possible, guarantees of lasting and profitable commercial relations. This had not been, and was not to be, the usual trend of French imperial economic policy. Leroy-Beaulieu also argues against the French tendency to excessive centralization, and expresses admiration for what he regards as the supple, realistic and empirical approach of the British. He finds the earlier French settlers adventurous, imaginative and good at improvisation, but (as against the British) somewhat amateur and impatient of gradual results. This respect for British methods, not untypical of some pragmatically-minded Frenchmen at some periods of French history, could be freely expressed because Leroy-Beaulieu was writing before the resentful suspicion of British policy which accumulated in France in the 'eighties, after the British occupation of Egypt, and remained acute until the *Entente Cordiale*.

It is noteworthy that, though Leroy-Beaulieu insists on the need for colonies to be given increasing independence by the mother country, he seems very little concerned with their effects on the independence of indigenous peoples. His subject was, of course, colonization, not imperialism; he approaches the question throughout from the point of view of the metropolitan race and of its branches overseas. Presumably he was against the extermination of 'natives' (Ferry certainly was) and in favour of dispossessing them as little as possible. Perhaps he assumed that, where such dispossession was necessary, the victims would be recompensed by their exposure to higher civilization. His general attitude suggests that his views on this topic would not be narrowly illiberal; at one point he writes approvingly of the admission of Indians to the councils of the *Raj;* but the problem was clearly not one that preyed on his conscience.

Although this work may have had an influence on French policy, it was not really in the mainstream of French imperial thought. For one thing there is little sign in it of a positive interest in 'missionary' achievement. This aspect of colonialism seems to have weighed more heavily with Ferry who, in a speech in the Senate on Algeria in 1891, proclaimed himself an advocate of gradual assimilation:

'J'ose dire que la politique française ayant toujours répudié avec honneur la colonisation par l'extermination, ayant également renoncé à la politique de refoulement, elle n'a, et ne peut avoir qu'une formule, c'est l'assimilation. . . . Assurément, l'assimilation au sens absolu, c'est l'oeuvre des siècles; mais l'oeuvre civilisatrice qui consiste à relever l'indigène, à lui tendre la main, à le civiliser, c'est l'oeuvre quotidienne d'une grande nation. . . .'

The end of the nineteenth century was the heyday of 'assimilation' in French imperial thought. The notion was applied too rigidly (and, inevitably, too superficially), so that it became discredited and gave way, before the First World War, to the more flexible theory of 'association'. Within limits, however, the tendency of the French Empire was at all times assimilatory. Indeed this was probably its most striking single characteristic. The Empire formed, at almost every stage, a closed—or largely closed—economic and cultural system. Within this system a serious, though necessarily uneven, effort was made to produce educational uniformity in accordance with French standards and to offer political equality—as opposed to independence—as an eventual ideal. Colonial representation in the metropolitan parliament gave to the fabric a Roman touch, which was important in principle, however partial or inequitable it may have been in practice.

The Colonial Congress of 1889 declared in its final resolution: 'All the efforts of colonization must tend to propagate amongst the natives our language, our methods of work, and gradually the spirit of our civilization.' More than half a century later the Brazzaville Conference pronounced against political or cultural autonomy for the colonies.

Deschamps[1] described assimilation as a 'tendency natural to the Latin and Christian French mind.' Historically it was a legacy from Imperial and, later, Catholic Rome; geographically it was an attitude more natural to a continental than to an insular people.

[1] *The French Union.*

Jacques Stern wrote in 1944, in a passage typical of French imperial sentiment:

'In contrast to the British, Dutch, Spanish and Portuguese, the French, whose attitude towards the natives is one of affection, pursued a policy tending towards eventual equality for them. In the nineteenth century we applied a system which was unknown to the conquerors of the past because it was born of the French Revolution. In our colonies, basing ourselves on the humanitarian doctrine of friendly association and progressive assimilation, we carried out a programme of liberation and civilization. . . .'[1] He noted that, even under the *ancien régime*, the seventeenth century statutes for Madagascar, drafted under Colbert's supervision, had provided that no distinction should be made between the French and the natives.

Stern's reference to the French Revolution recalls that French missionary zeal could be laic as well as religious. A radical supporter of colonial expansion[2] approached the sublime in an article written in 1886:

'*La grandeur de la France est indispensable au progrès de l'humanité. C'est pourquoi j'approuve une politique qui unira sous le drapeau français 100 millions de défenseurs de la Révolution.*'

It is easy enough to criticize the theory, and still more the practice, of French imperial assimilation. It imposed an artificial pattern on the economic and political life of the colonies. When applied ruthlessly it could have a blighting effect on native culture. Those who were more or less fully assimilated were apt to prefer life in France to life in their own countries. The system did little (it was not, of course, meant to) to prepare the colonies to stand on their own feet when independence came. Moreover it was never more than superficially and unevenly applied.

One verdict on political assimilation between the wars, was that it was 'undoubtedly the least practical, the least progressive and even the least humanitarian of all the theories of colonial relationship.'[3] Cromer, writing before the First World War,

---

[1] *The French Colonies, Past and Future.*

[2] Léon Hugonnet in *Le Réveil National* quoted in *Jules Ferry et le Partage du Monde.*

[3] Roberts: *op. cit.:* p. 70.

although impressed by French 'social adaptability' and by the attractiveness of French civilization to 'Asiatics and Levantines', doubted whether in the end the French had had much more success than the British in really assimilating their subject races.

Yet those who have seen something of French-speaking Africa must admit that French assimilation has had some striking successes. Much of the criticism to which it has given rise should have been directed at its rigid application rather than at the doctrine itself. It was, of course, as Ferry recognized, a long-term policy; both its partisans and its opponents were apt to underestimate the length of time that successful assimilation would need. As it was, the experiment could not be pushed to a conclusion; but it lasted long enough to bear some fruit—and the assimilatory influence is still, discreetly, at work. Colonial representation in Paris may have been inconvenient; it may have had some farcical consequences; but the men who had been trained in this school helped to smooth the transition from Empire to independence.

Sceptical of the possibilities of assimilation, Cromer went so far as to say: 'Neither in French, British, nor, I think I may add, Russian possessions is there the least probability that the foreign will eventually supplant the vernacular languages.' Perhaps it is early to say that he has been disproved. But, after fifty years, the hold of the imperial languages does not look like being too ephemeral.

Assimilation was not, of course, the beginning and end of French colonial policy. The project of Napoleon III for an 'Arab Kingdom' in Algeria, Lyautey's 'Indirect Rule' methods in Morocco and Faidherbe's prevention of European land settlement in Senegal were cases when the protection of subject races was preferred to their conversion. The French have also shewn, on occasions, a capacity for reverse assimilation. It is a commonplace that the French tend to be less racially exclusive than some other peoples. This can, of course, be exaggerated; there may not be a great deal to choose between an ordinary French settler family and a British in this respect. But it is probably true that French behaviour towards 'natives' has been, by

c   33

and large, less formal. Sexual liaisons seem to have been more frequent and have certainly been more open.[1] Champlain told the Canadian Indians: 'Our boys will marry your girls and we will be one people'; the *coureurs des bois*, unlike the more stationary English colonists, apparently inter-married freely; in all parts of the world it was better to be a half-caste in the French than in the British territories. According to Deschamps, Champlain and Brazza would sometimes live and dress native fashion; Dupleix and his wife, the Begum Johanna, demanded the honours due to Hindu princes; 'Laborde became a Malagasy prince, Lagarde an Abyssinian duke, Lyautey wanted to be buried under a Moroccan "koubba" '. French colonial literature is particularly rich in studies of native psychology. Against this background the peculiar fascination that the exploits of Lawrence of Arabia have had for many Frenchmen is no surprise.

After the generalizations, the usual doubts and exceptions occur. There are many strands in French civilization, many facets to 'the French temperament'. But it remains true that, on the whole, the attitude of French colonial administrators was less detached than that of the British; they were at once keener to influence and readier to be influenced. They were less fitted for, and less content with, the aloof role of the referee.

5. THE BRITISH APPROACH

All the six motives outlined at the beginning of this chapter are found in the making of the British Empire, though the 'Leadership Motive' was hardly important before the closing decades of the nineteenth century.

The 'Colonizing Motive' led the way in some of the more temperate parts of the Empire. It caused, notably, the Puritan settlements in New England, the Quaker settlements in Pennsylvania, and the settlement of loyalists in Nova Scotia after the American Revolution. From the end of the eighteenth century criminals were transported to Australia 'to remove the incon-

---

[1] Cf. p. 67 below.

venience which arose from the crowded state of the gaols'.[1] There was planned colonization of Australia and New Zealand, partly under Wakefield's inspiration, in the early nineteenth century.

The 'Economic Motive' was still more important. It lay at the bottom of early ambitions to discover a North-West Passage or to secure a share in the Spanish spoils of the New World. It was the motive of the London Company's expedition to Virginia under James I and of the exploitation of the West Indies. It caused the East India Company to adventure to India and the English Adventurers to trade into Hudson's Bay. It was trade, primarily, that brought about a British presence in West Africa and in South-East Asia; Singapore was occupied, in 1819, to break the commercial monopoly of the Dutch, with their Indonesian bases; Hong-Kong became a colony for the better protection of British merchants. Before the American Revolution Adam Smith wrote that the maintenance of commercial monopoly 'has hitherto been the principal, or more properly perhaps the sole end and purpose of the dominion which Great Britain assumes over her colonies'. Even in the hey-day of Free Trade, commerce was a spur to imperial effort. As late as 1860 Palmerston wrote in a Foreign Office minute that the extension of our West African trade was 'an object which ought to be actively and perseveringly pursued' and that, if necessary, a 'physical effort' should be made to protect it.

The 'Aggressive Motive' appealed less to the shop-keeping instinct. But a sense of adventure and romance inspired the early mariners and the nineteenth century African explorers. Raleigh and Gilbert seem to have dreamt of power in the New World as well as profit. (For that matter power and profit, in the mercantilist age, could appear as two sides of the same coin. Alexander Dalrymple, a former employee of the East India Company, wrote in 1769 that trade with the Australian continent would 'maintain the power, dominion and sovereignty of Britain'.) Adam Smith, attacking the mercantilist system, argued that such forms of dominion were unprofitable, but recognized that the surrender of authority over colonies would be mortifying to national pride.

[1] King's Speech at the opening of Parliament in 1787.

Warren Hastings was a man of large and cultivated views, who saw in India a 'temporary possession'; he was also, as the servant of the East India Company, the agent of an avowedly commercial enterprise. But he was neither above nor below a strain of high patriotism, evidently coloured by his classical and oriental studies. He wrote to Sir John Macpherson in 1782: 'It is now my most confirmed opinion that I should have drawn out of the first Scrapes of Bombay (had they committed no more) the Means of raising the British Empire in India to a Height of more splendid Glory, and a Greatness more permanent than any foreign State ever yet acquired over remote Provinces'.[1]

In the eighteenth century and earlier the power and prestige of Empire, if dear to the national pride, were still dearer to the royal honour. As Empire swelled or shrank, so did the royal estate. Colonel Simcoe wrote to Sir Joseph Banks in 1791, in terms which perhaps already seemed old-fashioned: 'I would die by more than Indian torture to restore my King and his family to their just inheritance and to give my country that fair and natural accession of power which an union with their brethren could not fail to bestow and render permanent'.[2] George III struggled to retain the American colonies as part of his 'just inheritance'. Queen Victoria had as strong a relish for her imperial titles, but less power to direct imperial policy.

The 'Strategic Motive' seemed particularly important in the shadow cast by the Napoleonic Wars, but it could never be ignored. Much of the British Empire was acquired in the eighteenth and early nineteenth century because, or in the course, of Anglo-French conflict. Commercial rivalry may in turn have helped to motivate this conflict. But it was only because the rivalry sharpened into war, that the British began to develop their military power in India. The Heights of Abraham were stormed during the Seven Years' War. Castlereagh occupied the Cape, in 1806, in order to prevent Holland, Napoleon's ally, from interfering with British trade. The extension of British rule in India in the decades before the Mutiny was partly strategic, and

---

[1] Letters edited by Professor Dodwell: p. 151.
[2] Quoted in *Concept of Empire*.

partly aggressive, in impulse. The strategic value of some of the smaller colonies was always apparent. The French, and subsequently the British, occupied Mauritius because it lay on the Indian route. Concern for the Indian route lay at the heart of British strategy both before and after 1870. To this extent the 'Strategic Motive', in spite of its importance, must rank as less basic than the motives—economic, aggressive or altruistic—which prompted the retention of the Indian Empire.

The 'Missionary Motive', both in the British and French Empires, usually contributed towards, rather than originated, imperial action. But it played its part from the beginning. According to Hakluyt's *Voyages* Mr. Edward Hay, who accompanied Sir H. Gilbert in his voyage to the New World in 1583, thought that 'the discoverie and planting' of remote countries could only succeed if their chief intent was the sowing of Christian religion, though 'reliefe of sundry people within this realme distressed' was also an honourable purpose. Sir Robert Heath, granted the first Carolina charter in 1629, was described as being 'kindled with a certain laudable and pious desire as well of enlarging the Christian religion as our Empire and increasing the Trade and Commerce of this our kingdom'.

The missionary and the settler were often at odds; but there was a close alliance, throughout, between the missionary and the trader; thus the 'Economic' and 'Missionary' motives went frequently hand-in-hand. In some of the American colonies, as later in South Africa and New Zealand, missionary activity tended to support native peoples against colonial encroachment. But in other parts of the world the influence of the missionaries was expansive, as they worked—in the spirit of Livingstone—to bring honest trade and the Word of God to 'heathen' peoples. Their influence was most marked in the earlier part of the nineteenth century, when there was a stronger proselytizing element in British Imperialism than at any other time. It was, of course, a missionary aim to replace the slave trade by legitimate commerce. Sir J. Banks, writing to Lord Liverpool in 1799, urged an expedition to the Niger for a nice mixture of commercial and philanthropic reasons: '. . . in a very few years a trading company might be established under immediate control of the Government, who could take upon themselves the whole expense of the measure, would govern the Negroes far more mildly and make them far more happy than they are now under the tyranny of their arbitrary princes, would become popular at home by converting them to the Christian Religion, by inculcating in their rough minds the mild morality which is engrafted on the tenets of our faith and by effecting the greatest practicable diminution of the Slavery of Mankind, upon the principles of natural justice and commercial benefit.'

The 'Missionary Motive' was seldom strong enough by itself to prompt the annexation of territory, though it often re-enforced the case for giving governmental support to traders. However, there were occasions when it was the direct cause of expansion. Sierra Leone was founded for philanthropic reasons, in 1787, by the Abolition of Slavery Society. Efforts to root out the Slave Trade, throughout the nineteenth century, involved strong measures on the West and East Coasts of Africa. The great Zanzibar slave-market was shut down in 1873 after the Sultan was faced with the threat of a blockade by the Royal Navy. Nothing is more striking in British history than the expense and energy devoted to the eradication of a trade which, in the eighteenth century, had made Liverpool and Bristol rich; there is no instance of humanitarian principles having so direct and sustained an effect on our overseas policies. The abolitionists were single-minded men who succeeded in imparting to official and public opinion their own absolute conviction of the rightness of their cause. It was not surprising that this conviction should be strong; but, even apart from slavery, no later Imperialist could quite reproduce the moral certainty and optimism of the early nineteenth century evangelicals. Wilberforce asked rhetorically in the House of Commons in 1813:

'. . . Are we so little aware of the vast superiority even of European laws and institutions, and far more of British laws and institutions, over those of Asia, as not to be prepared to predict with confidence, that the Indian community which should have exchanged its dark and bloody superstitions for the genial influence of Christian light and truth, would have experienced such an increase of civil order and security; of social pleasures and domestic comforts, as to be desirous of preserving the blessings it should have acquired; and can we doubt that it would be bound even by the ties of gratitude to those who had been the honoured instruments of communicating them?'

In the same spirit, and at about the same time, Sir Stamford Raffles, the founder of Singapore and an ally of the evangelical party, wrote:

'It is to British manners and customs that all nations now conform themselves. . . . It appears that there is something in our national character and condition which fits us for this exalted station. I think too that there is a kind of destination of this character and condition to this service. It was the privilege of Britain to receive first the purest beams of reformed religion.'[1]

British missionary zeal, when present, was usually religious. Even the creed of the Manchester School was not quite such a source of fervour as were, for the French radical, the principles of the Revolution. However, a note of eighteenth century humanism appears in the following passage by Henry Beaufoy (although a Quaker), who was the first secretary of the Association for Promoting the Discovery of the Interior Parts of Africa, founded in 1788:

'In pursuit of these advantages . . . [the extension of the Commerce and the encouragement of the Manufactures of Great Britain] . . . by means as peaceful as the purposes are just, the conveniences of civil life, the benefits of the mechanic and manufacturing arts, the attainments of science, the energies of the cultivated mind and the elevation of the human character may in some degree be imparted to nations hitherto consigned to hopeless barbarism and uniform contempt.'[2]

There was a missionary element, though a lay one, in the Whiggish itch to export the blessings of liberty and Free Trade. The 'Opium War' of 1839–40 did not aim at territorial aggrandise-

---

[1] Quoted in Knorr's *British Colonial Theories: 1580–1850*.
[2] Cited, together with the quotation from Sir J. Banks above, in an article by Robin Hallett in the *Journal of African History*, Vol. IV, 1963, No. 2.

ment (though it resulted in the cession of Hong Kong), but was none the less aggressive in its design to force commercial and diplomatic intercourse on an unwilling China. Palmerston is particularly associated with this type of policy, half-liberal and half-imperialist, but wholly imperialist in its assumption of a right to impose the standards of European liberalism on uncivilized, or reactionary, peoples. I have already quoted one Palmerstonian minute.[1] Another (December 20, 1850) speaks of '. . . wishing most earnestly that civilization may be extended in Africa, being convinced that commerce is the best pioneer of civilization, and being satisfied that there is room enough in. . . . Africa for the commerce of all the civilized nations of the rest of the world. . . .' Palmerston never seems to have had any doubts; but he was lucky enough to be swimming with the exhilarating current of expansive Liberalism. The water was colder, the climate less genial, for the later Imperialists.

Another lay missionary, of a later generation, was Winwood Reade, the traveller in West and Equatorial Africa. Reade rejected Christianity and revered the *Origin of the Species*. His evolutionary enthusiasm belonged to the end of the century; but he recalled the beginning in his belief in the assimilability of the Negro and in the Whiggish grounds on which he justified Empire. In *The Martyrdom of Man* (1872) he refutes the 'sickly school of politicians who declare that all countries belong to their inhabitants and that to take them is a crime'. This reads like a *fin-de-siècle* writer. But he regards Empire as a means, not an end:

'The great Turkish and Chinese Empires, the lands of Morocco, Abyssinia and Thibet, will be eventually filled with free, industrious and educated populations. But these people will never begin to advance until their property is rendered secure, until they enjoy the rights of man; and these they will never obtain except by means of European conquest'. And again:

'. . . The masses of the people [in Asia] are invariably slaves. The conquest of Asia by European powers is therefore in reality Emancipation, and is the first step towards the establishment of oriental nationality.'

[1] P. 35 above.

As I have already suggested, the 'Leadership Motive' was little in evidence in the period—up till about 1870—of which I am now writing. Imperial motives were either frankly selfish or, when altruistic, had a touch of 'missionary' fervour. However, in practice British colonial administrators were no doubt more concerned to govern than to proselytize. Similarly, those who felt a desire to justify the British Empire in India did not need to detect the dawn of enlightenment there. They could simply point to the anarchy which, it was already believed, would follow the Empire's collapse.

By the middle of the nineteenth century all of these motives were, relatively, in abeyance. Emigration was heavy, particularly from Ireland; but the existing colonies of British settlement seemed to offer, together with the U.S.A., enough space for it. Interest, even in these colonies, was spasmodic, most informed people assuming that they would follow their American predecessors into independence in due course. There was sometimes pressure by business interests for advance. The sad experience of the Colonial Office was expressed by an official in 1856:[1]

'Merchants press upon us new settlements that they may try their own experiments, it is unpopular to resist and we can always be inundated with evidence of the value of any spot on the Globe, or of its importance to national greatness—but after a time we are liable to find ourselves burdened with barren islands like the Falklands or unhealthy jungles like Labuan.'

On the whole, however, the triumph of Free Trade over Mercantilism, combined with world-wide British commercial and industrial success, had greatly weakened the force of the 'Economic Motive'. The 'Aggressive Motive' never quite died, but was blunted by the economic and moral complacency of the mid-Victorian intelligentsia. Cobden hoped to kill it with Manchester principles: 'The Colonial system', he declared in 1842, 'with all its dazzling appeal to the passions of the people, can never be got rid of except by the indirect process of free-trade'. The *Don Pacifico* incident of 1850 seemed to shew that the

---

[1] Quoted in *Verandah* by J. Pope-Hennessy: p. 58.

Englishman's prestige was sufficiently assured, even in *foreign* lands. The house of a Portuguese money-lender, who happened to have been born in Gibraltar, had been pillaged in Athens. This came as the culminating incident of a series of difficulties and Palmerston ordered a blockade of the Greek coasts. Defending his action in the Commons, he perorated:

'As the Roman, in the days of Rome, held himself free from indignity, when he could say *'Civis Romanus sum'*, so also a British subject, in whatever land he may be, shall feel confident that the watchful eye and the strong arm of England will protect him against injustice and wrong.'

The 'Strategic Motive' lay dormant, because the needs of British naval power, which was in any case not seriously challenged at this time, were already met. There was still an urge to proselytize. But attempts to convert the world to Free Trade seldom involved the formal extension of Empire. Free Trade apart, people were beginning to realize that it was going to be harder to proselytize than they had thought; progress looked like being a disappointingly acquired taste. The Indian Mutiny of 1857 was discouraging. In the 'sixties there were attacks on sentimental colonization.[1] Lord Stanley asserted, in 1865, that philanthropic endeavour at Sierra Leone 'had produced a race the most worthless of any in the world' and challenged the view 'that in some way or other we are responsible for the fortunes and destiny of the African race'.

During this period the principles of Gladstonian finance were in their prime. Financial economy was, as ever, a powerful opponent of Imperialism. The future of Canada was the most prominent imperial problem; its defence both cost money and carried the risk of an unwanted war with the U.S.A.

The distaste felt for Empire was mainly of a negative character. It was held to be expensive and unprofitable; it should be kept to a decent minimum. But it does not seem to have inspired any sense of shame. Nor were the subject peoples—when their reactions were considered at all—felt to suffer wrong. Most people probably thought them lucky to be exposed to civilization,

[1] Cf. *Prelude to the Partition of West Africa* by J. D. Hargreaves: pp. 27-28.

whether they appreciated it or not. Adam Smith, writing of the Spanish colonization of America, had referred to 'the injustice of coveting the possession of a country whose harmless natives, far from having ever injured the people of Europe, had received the first adventurers with every mark of kindness and hospitality. . . .' Scruples of a more businesslike kind tended to deter the mid-Victorians from imperial advance.

These were, of course, the days when India was the only large tropical dependency. Few cared to predict its future. Macaulay and Sir T. Munro had contemplated its eventual separation on, they hoped, friendly terms, Later in the century there seems to have been a kind of tacit agreement not to look too far ahead; meanwhile, the commercial advantages of the connection apart, it was unthinkable to abandon the continent to anarchy. The colonies of white settlement were either in sight of, or on the way to, full self-government. By the end of the 'sixties the North American and Australasian colonies were nearly as completely self-governing, in internal matters, as Great Britain. The Crown Colonies, on the other hand, were destined for occupation so long as they were needed for strategic or commercial purposes. Sir C. Adderley thought the Crown Colony system of government suitable for 'stations merely occupied for war, depots of trade and subjects of inferior race'. But the number of Crown Colonies must not be allowed to expand, except for compelling reasons.

The middle 'sixties marked the apex of this passive attitude towards the Empire. The radical intellectual Goldwin Smith, writing in his *Reminiscences* of the early 'sixties, recalled: 'Of the few people in England who thought about colonial subjects in my day, the general opinion was that the destiny of the colonies was independence.' The last trace of Mercantilism disappeared with the removal of the Timber Imperial Duty in 1866. The Ionian Islands were released from British protection, and united to Greece, in 1864. In 1865, a select Parliamentary Committee recommended a change of policy towards the West African Settlements, with a view to an ultimate withdrawal from all, except probably Sierra Leone. According to the Committee the object of policy should be to encourage those qualities in the native peoples which would 'make it possible for us more and more to transfer to them the administration of all the government'. The West African settlements, with their unattractive climate, seemed the least likely to be regretted of all the colonies. Lord Clarendon told H. M. Ambassador at the Hague: 'There is no care in this country for our African possessions. I believe that an announcement to get rid of them would be popular. . . .' It would certainly have been popular with Lord Stanley, who said: 'I do not believe there is a year or even a month that passes in which the service on that coast does not put an end to some life among our officers which, measured by any rational standard of comparison, is worth more than the merely animal existence of a whole African tribe.' (This passage shews that the language of withdrawal could be even loftier than that of expansion.) Nevertheless, when it came to the point, any proposal to discard a colony brought humanitarian and commercial pressure groups into action. The West African settlements remained and expanded; precious lives went on being buried in 'The White Man's Grave'.

Adam Smith and Cobden had been right. Underneath the attitudes of the intelligentsia the notion of Empire still had a hazy popular appeal; the possibility of withdrawal tended to make it articulate. Trollope, a particularly humane observer of colonial problems, himself a believer in eventual separation, wrote in 1859: 'A wish that British North America should ever be so severed from England . . . will by many Englishmen be deemed unpatriotic'.[1] The Liberal Henry Seymour said in the House of Commons in 1864: '. . . the natural course of a people so powerful, vigorous and enterprising as that of England was to expand and occupy nearly every region of the world. . . .'[2] Even the doldrums of the 'sixties were disturbed by breezes from past and future Imperialism.

A survey of British imperial advance before 1870 confirms that, if not exactly conceived in 'a fit of absence of mind', it was due to the presence of mind of individuals rather than to long-term

[1] Quoted in Bodelsen's *Studies in Mid-19th Century Imperialism:* p. 51.
[2] Hargreaves *op. cit.:* p. 71.

central planning. Imperial strategy may, exceptionally, have been viewed as a whole during the Seven Years' War; the strategic needs of the Empire were certainly in the minds of the British peace-makers after Napoleon's defeat; but no British Government either then or later sat round a table and said: 'Let's build an Empire'. When the Government acted it did so in response to a specific challenge or need. The humane, rather cynical, slightly dilettante, attitude of the Colonial Office officials illustrates the way in which Government approached colonial problems during most of the nineteenth century. At their back were the pressure groups, both commercial and humanitarian, who (except when strategic interests were at stake) were the usual authors of imperial expansion; behind them was the intelligentsia, frequently committed to doctrines in which Empire had little place; behind them again was the mass of uninformed opinion, ready to take a human pride in achievement and dominion, but seldom willing to make great sacrifices for them.

Such were, in brief, the motives of British empire-building before the last quarter of the nineteenth century. The Empire once built, how did the British approach the task of ruling foreign races?

In the eighteenth century British rule in India shewed traces of 'assimilation in reverse'. The East had always enjoyed a reputation for assimilating its conquerors. The early traders found themselves in the presence of a civilization that may have been decadent, but was elaborate and polite. Warren Hastings, although a British patriot, was the most enlightened and successful exponent of this attitude. He cultivated Asiatic learning and respected Indian manners; he wrote to Lord Mansfield in 1774 that he 'desired to found the authority of the British Government in Bengal on its ancient laws', his aim being 'to rule this people with ease and moderation according to their own ideas, manners and prejudices'. James Mill, although he had been critical of Hastings' conduct, said: 'He was the first, or among the first, of the servants of the Company, who attempted to acquire any language of the natives, and who set on foot those liberal enquiries into the language and literature of the Hindus, which have led to the satisfactory knowledge of the present day . . . his administration assuredly was popular, both with his countrymen and the natives of Bengal'. Macaulay regarded Hastings as hard and unscrupulous, and thought him 'inclined to overrate the value of his favourite studies', but had to admit: 'Even now, after the lapse of more than fifty years, the natives of India still talk of him as the greatest of the English. . . .'

The Indian influence was even exerted on the imperial country. The returning Nabobs brought back Indian wealth and some Indian habits. Thomas and William Daniell published aquatints of Indian buildings and scenery at the end of the eighteenth century. There were translations of Indian religious works and Indian echoes in English poetry. This was part of a movement that continued, gently, throughout the nineteenth century, spawning a wide range of aesthetic delights, from the transformation of Brighton Pavilion by John Nash in 'the Indian taste', to the 'Indian Love Lyrics' of the amateur singer's repertoire.

But the trial of Warren Hastings, insofar as it had any serious justification, suggested growing disapproval of the idea that Englishmen should go out to India to rule it in an Indian way, or that they should return infected with the political or private vices of the Orient. The scale of British operations in India had reached a point where the public conscience could no longer ignore them; there was an uneasy feeling that the East must not be allowed to corrupt traditional British ideas of justice, simplicity and freedom. Over a century later one of the grounds on which Hobson attacked Imperialism was that it favoured 'forms of political tyranny and social authority which are the deadly enemies of effective liberty and equality.'

In India itself the example set by Hastings was not long followed, perhaps partly because of the effect of his trial. His successors were on the whole less well versed in Indian culture and not so sympathetic to the Indian point of view. There began to be less mixing in society, particularly once increasing numbers of European women came out to join their husbands and fiancés

As British power in India grew, there was a natural tendency to be less impressed by the pomp of the enfeebled princes (though royalty would usually strike some kind of chord in British breasts). The evangelical influence did not encourage sympathy with Eastern morals. An Englishman noted in 1810 that, in Calcutta, 'Europeans have little connection with natives of either religion'. A senior lady, asked what she had seen of the country, replied with the complacent lethargy of a Jane Austen matron: 'Oh nothing, thank goodness. I know nothing at all about them, nor I don't wish to. Really I think the less one knows about them the better'.[1]

As the tide of 'assimilation in reverse' ebbed, it made way—at least in theory—for assimilation proper. I have already suggested that this was the most 'missionary' period of British imperial thought. Sir T. Munro, in his minute on the Employment of Natives in Public Service, written in 1824, put the case for educational progress with impressive sense and restraint:

'It ought undoubtedly to be our aim to raise the minds of the natives, and to take care that whenever our connection with India might cease, it did not appear that the only fruit of our dominion there, had been to leave the people more abject and less able to govern themselves than when we found them. . . . Liberal treatment has always been found the most effectual way of alleviating the character of many people, and we may be sure that it will produce a similar effect on that of the people of India. The change will no doubt be slow. . . .'

Macaulay told the House of Commons in 1833 that, if the day came when our subjects should demand European institutions, it would be 'the proudest day in English history. . . . There is an empire exempt from all natural causes of decay . . . that empire is the imperishable empire of our arts and our morals, our literature and our laws'. The following year he travelled to Madras as a member of the Supreme Council. There was a difference of opinion in the Committee of Public Instruction: half were for extending the old scheme of encouraging Oriental learning by stipends and grants; half were for teaching the elements of

[1] Both these quotations are from *British Social Life in India* by D. Kincaid.

knowledge in the vernacular tongues but the higher branches in English. The latter had been the view of Mountstuart Elphinstone, Governor of Bombay from 1819 to 1824; it was also Macaulay's —and his influence was decisive. He was convinced, in his dogmatic way, that the native languages offered 'no books on any subject which deserve to be compared to our own'. 'The languages of Western Europe civilized Russia. I cannot doubt that they will do for the Hindoo what they have done for the Tartar'.

The ideal of assimilation (or at least of partial assimilation) was not confined to India. There had at one time been hopes, in some quarters, of assimilating the French Canadians. Speaking of the population of Quebec in 1774 the Attorney-General told the Commons: 'When gentlemen apply the word 'assimilation' to religion, to law, to civil laws, and to manners, I can easily conceive it is not an undesirable object in policy that they should be so far assimilated. . . .' The missionaries were apt to be rather drastic assimilators the world over.[1] Gladstone preached a measure of political and social assimilation in 1855, when he told the Chester Mechanics Institute that the British should avail themselves 'in reason and moderation' of openings to reproduce 'the copy of those laws and institutions, those habits and national characteristics, which have made England so famous as she is'. Winwood Reade defended the concept of Negro assimilability:

'However ludicrous it may seem to hear a Negro boasting about Lord Nelson and Waterloo, and declaring that he must go home to England for his health, it shows that he possesses a kind of emulation, which, with proper guidance, will make him a true citizen of his adopted country, and leave him nothing of the African except his skin.'

Nevertheless, when the aim was assimilatory, its standard target was eventual liberty, under institutions of British form, rather than a permanent political connection within a centralized system based, in the French style, on the principle of equal

---

[1] Cf. *The Road to Self-Rule* by Prof. W. M. Macmillan: p. 85: 'Faced in the West Indies and in still newer countries, or even in India, with situations of the greatest social complexity, the missionaries did not set themselves to study customs but to uproot them, and to substitute Christian civilization as they knew it—the individual, fiercely competitive civilization of their homeland.'

rights. The ultimate destiny of the subject peoples would be, it was usually hoped, Christian, liberal and English-speaking; but not, in a political sense, British. As a general rule British ambition to assimilate was limited by attachment to the ideas of liberty and ultimate self-determination, by the example of the American colonies and by the Anglo-Saxon pride of race frequently observed, or exemplified, by Victorian writers. Macaulay himself referred to 'the pride of caste naturally felt by an Englishman in India'. Throughout the nineteenth century race-consciousness reinforced the tendency of the British overseas towards social exclusiveness and barred any really thorough attempts at assimilation. When the volatile Irish Anglophobe Pope-Hennessy arrived to govern Labuan and Hong-Kong (in the 'sixties and 'seventies) he noted, with disapproval, the lack of social mixing between the races. He also refused to accept the 'Superior Being' theory held by Europeans in the West African settlements. This was so radical a point of view that it moved a Liberal Colonial Secretary, Lord Kimberley, to write: 'It is impossible not to distrust the judgement of a man who can write in this strain.'

Together with 'missionary' optimism, the idea of assimilation declined, as a force in British imperial theory and practice, in the later nineteenth century. Twentieth century policies, designed to prevent detribalization and to promote 'Indirect Rule', were in some sort its antithesis. These policies, reacting against the ideals of expansive Liberalism, showed a tendency to revert, in different circumstances and in a different spirit, to the Warren Hastings technique. Perhaps they also reflected the emphasis on trusteeship, the concern to protect weaker races, which had seldom ceased to influence British official imperial policy. Even in the eighteenth century the British Government had sought to protect the Red Indians against the American colonists and the French Canadians against the British. Throughout the nineteenth century the Colonial Office, often in alliance with the missionaries, saw itself as the guardian of racial minorities and backward peoples. A Parliamentary Committee under the chairmanship of Sir T. Buxton enquired in the 'thirties into the state of the aborigines in the British settlements and recommended that their protection should be the prerogative of the imperial government, rather than of the colonial legislatures. The Committee's recommendations were not passed into law, but they helped to form Colonial Office practice. In 1882 Sir R. Herbert, the Permanent Under-Secretary, wrote of '. . . the ignorant and helpless Indian population [of Mauritius] which must be protected by the Crown as in every other Eastern Colony'. This paternalism may seem to some the main virtue of the gentlemanly, if sometimes lethargic, Colonial Office of the days before Joseph Chamberlain. Reinforced by other considerations it survived to colour the attitude of twentieth century British officials towards the Rhodesian question.

II

The New Imperialism

Towards the end of the nineteenth century a new mood of Imperialism began to invade the country. For the first time in British history, except during the American War of Independence, Empire became a vividly controversial question in internal politics; perhaps for the first time there were partisans of the idea of Empire in the abstract. The origins of this mood are usually traced back to about 1870. The date is, of course, an arbitrary one. During the 'seventies the British attitude towards Empire was gradually becoming less passive. The 'eighties was the chief decade of actual expansion and of competition with other European powers in Africa. It was not really until the 'nineties, and especially in the last years of the century (the years of the Boer War and of the new, popular, journalism) that Imperialism became a demagogic force.

It was in the nature of things that, sooner or later, people should begin to take a more active interest in the Empire than they had felt in the mid-Victorian period. The swing of the pendulum is not only felt in party politics; there must always be a reaction when political ideas and opportunites have been neglected or pushed too far. Dilke's *Greater Britain*, published in 1868, helped to stimulate interest in British achievements overseas. The inaugural meeting of the Royal Colonial Institute took place in May, 1869. In 1870 a working men's petition on behalf of emigration was presented to the Queen. Bodelsen has shewn in detail, in *Studies in Mid-Victorian Imperialism*, how much of this new activity was provoked by the belief that Gladstone's first, reforming, administration (1868–1874) was preparing to shed imperial responsibilities. In fact the Gladstone Government do not seem to have considered seriously the abandonment of any colony except in the case of the Gambia, and that as part of a bargain with France.[1] But there was a natural alliance between 'separatism' on the one hand and economy an reform on the other. Bodelsen cites instances of press criticism in 1869–1870. Perhaps the Government would have taken a more openly separatist line, if there had seemed less danger of public opposition.

It seems to have been about this time that the word 'Imperialism', in its present meaning, began to come into use. It had previously been roughly synonymous with 'despotism' or 'Czarism', and is so used by Dilke. An issue of the *Spectator*, in 1869, mentioned the spirit of Imperialism as having 'died out of Englishmen'. Although the new meaning was unfamiliar to Lord Carnarvon, Disraeli's Colonial Secretary, in 1878, Gladstone had employed it in 1877, when he referred in the *Nineteenth Century* to his political opponents as the party 'who at home as well as abroad are striving to cajole or drive us into Imperialism'. The word seems to have taken a long time to settle into its new meaning. As late as 1895 the *Westminster Gazette* recalled that Seeley's *Expansion of England* gave 'a decisive impulse to what may be called, in the slang of the day, "the new Imperialism" '.

The early Imperialist movement was, except for occasional apocalyptic glimpses of the future, relatively free from Jingoism. It was concerned with the colonies of British settlement and was less directed towards the expansion of Empire, than to the consolidation of imperial links. The *Oxford English Dictionary* of 1933, defining the new usage of 'Imperialism' as 'the principle or spirit of empire; advocacy of what are held to be imperial interests', distinguished two sub-meanings in 'recent British politics': the first, an expansive attitude towards Empire; the second, the movement towards greater imperial unity. It may be that, even in the 'eighties and 'nineties, the greater part of Imperialist propaganda fell under the second heading. Many, perhaps most, of the late Victorians who were seriously interested in the Empire

[1] In *The English in the West Indies*, however, Froude claims that 'a high colonial official' told him in 1870 that: 'Jamaica, Trinidad and the English Antilles were to be masters of their own destiny.'

had as their chief aim a strengthening of the links between the mother country and the existing colonies of British stock. This will be discussed more fully in the following chapters; meanwhile it is worth noting that, in practice, the two aspects of Imperialism were less distinct than in theory: an interest in one of them tended to involve interest in the other; most Imperialists came to regard most forms of imperial activity as good.

Gladstone accused the Disraeli Administration (1874–1880) of pushing the country into Imperialism. At first sight its record does look distinctly Imperialist:

1874 Annexation of Fiji;

1874 Gold Coast Protectorate annexed as Crown Colony;

1874 Treaty between the Straits Settlement Government and the Sultan of Perak leading to the appointment of a British Resident (this pointed the way to a further extension of British protection in Malaya);

1875 Purchase of shares in the Suez Canal;

1876 Royal Titles Bill, under which the Queen became Empress of India;

1877 Annexation of Transvaal;

1878 Acquisition of Cyprus;

1878 Wars against Afghans and Zulus;

1879 Anglo-French dual control of Egypt.

In fact, however, as the record of the succeeding Gladstone Administration tends to show, it was the pressure of events rather than an aggressive Imperialism that impelled the Disraeli Government forward. Fiji was annexed on invitation; the Gold Coast became a Crown Colony after an Ashanti War which the preceding Gladstone Government had launched; the Transvaal was annexed as part of a policy of federation which it was hoped would prepare the way for a reduction of British responsibilities in South Africa; the Afghan War was due to fears of Russian policy; action in Egypt—which it was left to Gladstone to occupy —was taken to protect the foreign bondholders. Gladstone would have taken a different line from Disraeli on the Eastern Question and would certainly not have acquired Cyprus; he would presumably never have bought the Suez Canal shares or sympathized with the Queen's desire to be crowned Empress of India. Otherwise there was much less to choose between the imperial policies of the two parties, and between the attitudes of their leading men towards imperial questions, than party polemics suggested. There was nothing eagerly expansionist in the temper of the Disraeli Administration. It refused to sponsor Stanley's ideas for the exploitation of Central Africa. It was reluctant to get involved in the imperial campaigns in South Africa and Afghanistan.[1]

Disraeli himself is at times represented as the arch-apostle of Imperialism and at others as a cynical exploiter of dawning imperial sentiment, who was secretly bored with colonial questions. He first came forward in public as an Imperialist in his famous Crystal Palace speech of 1872 which, for the first time, proposed the Conservatives as champions of Empire. In this speech he accepted the principle of self-government for the settlement colonies, but urged that it should have been granted under conditions which would have strengthened and clarified the imperial connection. He went on to say:

'The issue is not a mean one. It is whether you will be content to be a comfortable England, modelled and moulded upon Continental principles and meeting in due course an inevitable fate, or whether you will be a great country, an Imperial country, a country where your sons, when they rise, rise to paramount positions, and obtain not merely the esteem of their countrymen, but command the respect of the world.'

The sincerity of Disraeli's imperial sentiment is impugned partly because of his remark in a letter in 1852 that: 'These wretched Colonies will all be independent, too, in a few years, and are a millstone round our necks'. In the same vein he wrote to Derby in 1866, urging that a budget saving should be effected by giving up West Africa and by leaving the Canadians to defend themselves: 'Power and influence we should exercise in Asia; consequently in Eastern Europe, consequently also in Western Europe: but what is the use of these colonial deadweights which

[1] Cf. p. 89 below.

we do not govern?' In the light of these remarks Disraeli can be represented as cashing in, like an astute politician, on the public reaction to the supposedly separatist aims of the first Gladstone Government. But Disraeli was too imaginative not to have realized, long before 1872, the possibilities of the Empire both for the statesman and for the politician. In 1847 he had tentatively suggested an Imperial Union at Aylesbury; in 1851 he proposed to Derby the possibility of 'a great push . . . to re-construct our Colonial system, or rather Empire . . .'; in 1859 he said at Aylesbury that England was bound 'to the communities of the New World, and those great states which our own planting and colonizing energies have created, by ties and interests which will sustain our power and enable us to play as great a part in the times yet to come as we do in these days, and as we have done in the past'. The note of romantic ambition in the passage from the Crystal Palace speech quoted above is typical and sincere. As early as 1867 Sir J. Skelton formed the impression of Disraeli:

'. . . This mightier Venice—this Imperial Republic on which the sun never sets—that vision fascinates him, or I am much mistaken. England is the Israel of his imagination, and he will be the Imperial Minister, before he dies—if he gets the chance.'

The fact is that the imagination of Disraeli, like that of Curzon after him, responded more eagerly to Empire in the East, than to the development of free relations with the colonies of British stock. He was only really interested in these colonies insofar as they could be expected to contribute to British power and prestige. The Jew, the traveller in the Levant, the author of *Tancred*, had other dreams than that of consolidating the Anglo-Saxon race—fascinated though he was by the influence of race on world politics. He wanted to 'hold the gorgeous East in fee'. By the same token he preferred the methods of Empire to be gorgeous and oriental: the Royal Titles Bill was a late, but striking, example of 'assimilation in reverse'. But his main contribution to Imperialism was less fanciful: he never tired of insisting that, in foreign affairs, principle was not a substitute for power. Thus, although he died before the Imperialist fever was at its height, although he never developed his imperial vision in his writings as he had his Tory domestic philosophy, and although his own policy when in office was defensive rather than expansive, Disraeli's attitude to foreign affairs was much more in tune than Gladstone's with the approaching era of imperial struggle and scramble.

Hobson calculated that one-third of the Empire, in terms of territory, had been acquired within the last thirty years of the nineteenth century; but this seems to have been a loaded estimate. The main area of expansion was in East Africa and the main period of expansion was in the latter 'eighties. (As late as 1883 a textbook[1] could state that 'the policy of England discourages any increase of territory in tropical countries already occupied by native races'.) As we have already seen, French Imperialism took on a new lease of life in the early 'eighties. The great year of German expansion, in Africa and New Guinea, was 1884–1885. The main dates in British expansion, after 1880, were:

1881   Chartering of the North Borneo Company;
1882   Occupation of Egypt;
      National Africa Company chartered for operations on the lower Niger;
1885   Niger Coast Protectorate formed;
      Bechuanaland annexed (partly as a Colony and partly as a Protectorate);
1886   Annexation of Burma;
1888   Imperial British East Africa Company chartered to occupy Uganda (the territory was taken over by the British Government as a Protectorate in 1894);
1889   South Africa Company chartered (the beginnings of Rhodesia);
1891   Protectorate proclaimed over Nyasaland;
1896–9 Re-conquest of the Sudan.

This list, of course, simplifies a chain of happenings which was often very complex. It does not cover all the expansion that took place during this period, but only the more striking events. Two further dates of importance for the Empire were 1895, when J.

[1] Quoted by Dilke in *Problems of Greater Britain*.

Chamberlain went to the Colonial Office for a period of eight years, and the beginning of the Boer War in 1899.

What were the motives behind this expansion? One explanation, become almost classic, is that, although a number of motives were present, the determining factor was the commercial or financial interest of a restricted class of capitalists, merchants, servicemen and officials—and that this interest was opposed to that of the nation as a whole. This was the view presented by Hobson and Moon; in essence it can be traced back to Adam Smith's criticisms of the first British Empire.

But, in the last resort, imperial action during the 'eighties and early 'nineties was taken, or permitted, by the Government in Whitehall, and particularly by two aristocratic statemen: Salisbury and Rosebery. The reasons which they and other Ministers gave in public did not necessarily reflect the real pre-occupations of the Government. Recent research into official papers[1] suggests that it was the 'Strategic', not the 'Economic', motive that weighed most with Ministers and officials. (Throughout the British Empire's history strategic considerations had been the main cause of direct action by Government.) Salisbury, a diplomatist rather than an Empire-builder, was the dominant figure; his constant purpose to protect the existing national and imperial fabric, relying on his own realistic, even ruthless, intelligence and on the governing instinct of the English oligarchy. Expansion was never welcomed in Downing Street during these years. The prime object was defensive, as it had been under Disraeli: the prevention of serious inroads into British power; the anticipation of other powers, when strategically necessary, in the 'Scramble for Africa'; the protection of the route to India and the East. The safety of the Suez Canal had already become a cardinal point of British policy.

Of course Ministers had to take public opinion into account; but the expansion of the 'eighties took place before the more Jingo mood of the turn of the century and, even then, there was no eagerness in Parliament for imperial expenditure. Of course they were subject, like the French and German Governments, to commercial pressure. In Nigeria and Nyasaland they did act,

[1] See *Africa and the Victorians* by Robinson, Gallagher and Denny.

though reluctantly, to protect existing spheres of commercial and missionary activity. Bechuanaland was annexed partly to forestall the Germans; partly to prevent its absorption by the Transvaal, which would have been unpopular with the missionaries and increased the power of the Boers in South Africa. But in East Africa the strategic motive of protecting the Canal, and with it the route to the East, was decisive and direct. It is remarkable how far the security of the Indian Empire appears to have dictated imperial policy. Although Seeley was not at all sure how profitable to Great Britain the Indian connection was, the need to protect it seems to have been regarded as the chief imperial requirement. Burma was annexed because of French activity in South-East Asia, in order to safeguard the approaches to India. Even the retention of imperial supremacy in South Africa, for the sake of which the government faced the Boer War, could appear, primarily, as a strategic interest. Hicks Beach said that the loss of supremacy there' . . . would mean the loss of the Cape of Good Hope, perhaps the most important strategical position in the world and one of the main links of our great Empire.'[1]

Particular frontiers were extended, or protected, for the sake of the rest of the Empire—and the heart of the rest was India. Chamberlain's desire to develop the country's 'tropical estates'; Rosebery's notion of 'pegging out claims for the future'(1893); the idea of using expansion as a solution to economic depression; all came too late to have much territorial effect. The *Economist* in 1892 thought that East Africa was 'probably an unprofitable possession'[2]; it was primarily for strategic reasons that the government held on to it.

The most enthusiastic case of expansion during this period was, in the British tradition, due to private enterprise. It seems unlikely that, without Rhodes, what is now Rhodesia would have been occupied by British settlers. But Rhodes was not really typical of his generation. Although he had fervent admirers, his approach was exceptional and his career unique. Such support as he obtained from the British Government was at least partly given because the effort to maintain imperial supremacy in South

[1] Quoted in *Africa and the Victorians*: p. 461. [2] *Africa and the Victorians*: p. 15.

Africa (for the sake of India and imperial strategy as a whole) seemed to depend on his help.

What other motives influenced late Victorian expansion? Froude advocated emigration; Lugard saw 'the teeming populations of Europe' turning to 'the fertile highlands of Africa to seek new fields of expansion'. Rhodesia and Kenya did in fact attract British settlers; yet, with the possible exception of Kenya, the 'Colonizing Motive' was hardly a determining factor. The 'Aggressive Motive' was certainly present in the popular mood, particularly at the turn of the century; but, as I have already suggested, it had little influence on official action. However, the refined versions of this motive, noted at the beginning of the last chapter,[1] became increasingly prominent in debate. Like the French we were afraid of losing our position as a first-class power—of being unable to measure up to Russia, the U.S.A. and perhaps Germany—if we lost our imperial position. Froude said: 'our place as a first-rate power is gone among such rivals unless we can identify the colonies with ourselves. . . .' Dilke was concerned to maintain Anglo-Saxon supremacy against Russia and, to a lesser extent, to keep a balance between the British Empire and the U.S.A. within the Anglo-Saxon world. Milner told the Manchester Conservative Club in 1906: 'These islands by themselves cannot always remain a Power of the very first rank'. The 'survival of the fittest' form of the 'Aggressive Motive' also had some theoretical importance. Hobson devoted a chapter to arguments of this kind. The *Origin of the Species* had appeared in 1859; talk of Race (witness Disraeli's 'All is race: there is no other truth') had for some time been fashionable. In his book *Social Evolution* (1894) Benjamin Kidd envisaged that the tropics should be administered—and their resources developed—from the temperate regions, on the ground that: 'the process which has gradually developed the energy, enterprise and social efficiency of the race northwards, and which has left less richly endowed in this respect the peoples inhabiting the regions where the conditions of life are easiest, is . . . part of the cosmic order of things which we have no power to alter'. Theories based on Evolution

[1] p. 16 above.

coloured the *fin-de-siècle* mood; but they had little practical effect on imperial expansion, except insofar as they influenced Rhodes in his dreams and actions.[1]

One exotic fruit on the Evolutionary branch of Aggressive Imperialism was a poem by John Davidson, *The Testament of an Empire Builder*, which was inspired by Rhodes' career and published in 1902. In this strange poem Davidson evokes the universal struggle for existence and pictures the 'happy slaughter of his enemies' as a necessary deed, which only Man's mouldering conscience has turned to mortal sin. Heaven is portrayed as full of the bold and enterprising, whether or not successful; Hell, which contains 'the greater part of all the swarthy all the tawny tribes', is given over to the weak, the timid, the altruistic, the poor in spirit. The Empire-Builder is made to say:

> *For me, I clambered into Heaven at once*
> *And stayed there; joined the warfare of the times*
> *In corner, trust and syndicate: upheaved*
> *A furrow, hissing through the angry world,*
> *A redshot ploughshare in a frozen glebe,*
> *And reaped my millions long before my prime.*
> *'Then, being English, one of the elect*
> *Above all folks, within me fate grew strong.*
> *The authentic mandate of imperial doom*
>
> .   .   .   .   .   .
>
> *Undid my simple, immature, design,*
> *And made me—what! Tenfold a criminal?*
> *No other name for Hastings, Clive and me!*
> *I broke your slothful dream of folded wings,*
> *Of work achieved and empire circumscribed,*
> *Dispelled the treacherous flatteries of peace,*
> *And thrust upon you in your dull despite*
> *The one thing needful, half a continent*
> *Of habitable land! The English Hell*
> *Forever crowds upon the English Heaven.*
> *Secure your birthright; set the world at nought;*

[1] Cf. p. 72 below.

THE NEW IMPERIALISM

Confront your fate; regard the naked deed;
Enlarge your Hell; preserve it in repair;
Only a splendid Hell keeps Heaven fair.'

If Rhodes' career was exceptional in British imperial practice, Davidson's ruthless tribute to him was still more exceptional in British imperial theory. It was more typical of *fin-de-siècle* aesthetics than politics.

The 'Missionary Motive' was seldom to the fore during this period. Missionary pressure contributed to expansion in Africa; but the missionaries seem to have been concerned with protecting native peoples, as much as with converting them. Eradication of the slave trade was still an important object, particularly in East Africa: according to his daughter this was Salisbury's 'only crusading impulse'. An unusually thorough attempt was made, after the annexation of Burma, to turn it into a modern state. On the whole, however, assimilatory techniques were not very actively pursued. In India the effect of the Mutiny had been to discourage the earlier crusading spirit, with its belief in the power of European progress to penetrate and improve. Bagehot, writing in 1869, reflected the decline in optimism: 'The experience of the English in India shows—if it shows anything—that a highly civilized race may fail in producing a rapidly excellent effect on a less civilized race, because it is too good and too different. . . . Consequently the two races have long lived together . . . separated by a whole era of civilization, and so affecting one another only a little in comparison with what might have been hoped.'

On the other hand, the 'Leadership Motive' acquired a new importance, whether as a contributory reason for expansion, or as a justification for it. As the difficulties of proselytism became more apparent, the moral impulse sought a fresh outlet. Experience in India suggested that, if the British could not, or would not, assimilate the Indians, at least they could keep order among them. Even critics of Imperialism tended to assume that 'backward' peoples were the better for civilized supervision. Hobhouse, writing in 1905, on the eve of the Liberal triumph, said: 'Until yesterday it was the opinion everywhere prevalent that the East was incapable of Self-Government'—and was still not quite certain of the contrary.

The masochistic appeal of the 'White Man's Burden' would have surprised some earlier builders of empire; but the new British Imperialists responded to it and were quietly convinced that their shoulders bore the burden best. A young Englishman in India wrote to his fiancée:[1]

'How is it that these pale-cheeked exiles give security to a race of another hue, other tongues, other religions which rulers of their own people have ever failed to give: Dearest, there are unseen moral causes which I need not point out. . . . .'

Dilke observed, in his more sophisticated way: 'Nature seems to intend the English for a race of officers, to direct and guide the cheap labour of the Eastern peoples.' Cromer urged his country-men not to 'weary in well-doing' in Egypt. Chamberlain, speaking at a Royal Colonial Institute dinner in 1897, regretted the blood-shed involved in imperial conquests, in bringing 'these countries into some kind of disciplined order', but added: '. . . it must be remembered that that is the condition of the mission we have to fulfil'. Milner believed the *Pax Britannica* to be 'essential to the maintenance of civilized conditions of existence among one-fifth of the human race' who lacked 'the gift of maintaining peace and order for themselves'. But perhaps the most complete statement of 'Leadership' Imperialism was given by Froude:[2]

'We have another function such as the Romans had. The sec-tions of men on this globe are unequally gifted. Some are strong and can govern themselves; some are weak and are the prey of foreign invaders and internal anarchy; and freedom, which all desire, is only attainable by weak nations when they are subject to the rule of others who are at once powerful and just. This was the duty which fell to the Latin race two thousand years ago. In these modern times it has fallen to ours, and in the discharge of it the highest features in the English character have displayed themselves'.

[1] Quoted in *British Social Life in India:* p. 204.
[2] *The English in the West Indies* (1888): p. 182.

This is all strong stuff; but it is no stronger than passages already quoted from Raffles, Wilberforce and other early or middle nineteenth century figures. The more one studies late Victorian expansion, the less it seems the result of a new surge of pride, self-confidence or conscious strength. In a sense Palmerston was more expansive than any late Victorian statesman; if anything he was even more convinced of national superiority. But the lack of competition in the mid-Victorian era (France politically divided; Russia despotic; Germany still forming; the U.S.A. on the verge of Civil War) helped British Governments to get their way by influence, rather than by power. During this period, British interests and principles coincided in the happiest way. The lion was at his most superior; but too well-fed to look crudely for prey.

After the defeat of Napoleon, British insularity, reinforced by the revival of Puritan spirit, as well as by political success at home and commercial success abroad, created an extraordinarily strong and complacent sense of national superiority which survived, in a muted form, until well into the twentieth century. Some random quotations from imperially-minded writers and speakers, apart from those already given, may help to illustrate this continuing mood:

'To the English People in World History. . . . There have been, shall I prophesy, two grand tasks assigned: Huge-looming through the dim tumult of the always incommensurable Present Time, outlines of two tasks disclose themselves: the grand industrial task of conquering some half or more of this terraqueous planet for the use of man; then secondly, the grand Constitutional task of sharing in some pacific endurable manner, the fruit of said conquest, and showing all people how it might be done.'

(CARLYLE: from *Chartism*)

The noblest men methinks are bred
Of ours the Saxon-Norman race. . . .
(TENNYSON: from the unpublished version of
To the Queen: 1851)

'Love of race, among the English, rests upon a firmer basis than love of mankind or love of Britain, for it reposes upon a subsoil of things known; the ascertained virtues and powers of the English people.'

(DILKE: from *Greater Britain*)

'We have conquered our present position because the English are a race of unusual vigour both of body and mind— industrious, energetic, ingenious, capable of great muscular exertion, and remarkable along with it for equally great personal courage.'

(FROUDE: from *England and the Colonies*)

'There is a destiny now possible to us, the highest ever set before a nation to be accepted or refused. We are still undegenerate in race; a race mingled of the best northern blood. . . . This is what England must either do, or perish; she must found colonies as fast and as far as she is able, formed of her most energetic and worthiest men; . . . their first aim is to be to advance the power of England by land and sea. . . .'

(RUSKIN: from his inaugural lecture at Oxford: 1870)

'We happen to be the best people in the world, with the highest ideals of decency and justice and liberty and peace, and the more of the world we inhabit, the better it is for humanity.'

'. . . Those who I think are the greatest people the world has ever seen, but whose fault is that they do not know their strength, their greatness and their destiny.'

(RHODES)

'. . . The greatest secular agency for good that the world has seen. . . .'

(ROSEBERY on the British Empire: 1884)

'I believe that the British race is the greatest of governing races that the world has ever seen.'

(CHAMBERLAIN, at the Imperial Institute: 1895)

'. . . The Englishman, amidst many deviations from the path, will strive, perhaps to a greater extent than any other member of that [the European] family, to attain to a high degree of eminently Christian civilization. . . .'

'. . . Worthy of the past history, the might, the resources, and the sterling national qualities of the Anglo-Saxon race.'

(CROMER: from *Modern Egypt*).

It is unfair to take such passages out of context; yet perhaps their combined effect is moving, as well as distasteful. The feeling of pride, however intolerable to others, was genuine and, in part, justified. It was no stronger at the end of the century than towards the beginning. It became noisier, less effortless, less optimistic. But the basic emotion was no more powerful.

At the same time, the note of anxiety discernible in Ruskin's inaugural lecture became more general. Tennyson echoed it in the Epilogue to the *Idylls of the King*, where he attacked the suggestion that Canada might leave the Empire (Lord Dufferin wrote from Ottawa, early in 1873, to thank him for these lines):

> *Is this the tone of empire? here the faith*
> *That made us rulers? . . .*
> > *The Loyal to the Crown*
> *Are loyal to their own far sons, who love*
> *Our ocean-empire with her boundless homes*
> *For ever-broadening England, and her throne*
> *In our vast Orient, and one isle, one isle,*
> *That knows not her own greatness; if she knows*
> *And dreads it we are fall'n. . . .*

In the parliamentary debate on the annexation of Fiji, the Under-Secretary ventured to hope 'not only that we should not abandon our Colonies, but that we should not abandon colonization, for such abandonment had usually been, if he read history aright, the precursor of a period of national decay.'[1] A similar warning would surely have sounded oddly earlier in the century. Foreign competition and the imposition of

---

[1] Quoted in the *Cambridge History*, Vol. III: p. 45.

foreign tariffs gradually made the country aware that British principles were not going to triumph automatically. Bismarck, Majuba and the fall of Khartoum helped to awaken Englishmen to the realities of power. Notions of racial superiority tended to become less benevolent and more precise. Both Raffles and Rhodes thought that the British people were fitted for their 'exalted station' by something in the national character; both may have seen the hand of God in this; but, with Rhodes, it was Race, not Religion, that took the first place. In the last years of the century, and particularly under the strain of the Boer War, popular Imperialism, spurred on by the newly sensational Press, was apt to betray a kind of hysteria, which suggested decadence rather than growth. Whether it revealed a real decadence or simply a cheapening of taste, the mood of extreme Jingoism was not long-lived. But the days of Empire, too, were numbered. It was not the bugle-call of imperial effort that was being sounded, but the first, raucous, notes of its swan song.

The mood of popular Imperialism was a new one; but it was only a version—either more vulgar or less confident—of an existing sense of national pride. It was never universal and it never had much direct influence on events. What was perhaps more important, for the half-century of Empire still ahead, was the growth of a serious and informed interest in imperial affairs. Seeley noted, in his *Expansion of England*, that, a generation ago, it had been 'the reigning opinion that there is nothing good in politics but liberty. . . .' Once the hold of liberal theory began to weaken, it was natural that intelligent men should start to take a positive pride in the Empire and to explore its possibilities. As communications improved imperial travel became more normal. Dilke and Froude both travelled widely in the Empire. Rosebery's visit to Australia in 1883 confirmed him in his Imperialism; subsequently he visited India and Egypt. According to his biographer[1] Chamberlain's visit to Egypt in 1889 at the age of 54 '—marked an epoch in his mind . . . widened and established his faith. A new revelation of Britain's organizing power in the East made him whole as an imperialist.'

[1] Garvin's *Life of Joseph Chamberlain*, Vol. II: p. 447.

As we shall see, the more responsible advocates of Imperialism remained relatively free from crude Jingoism in their outlook and language, though their claims are likely to seem excessive today. Their writings and speeches set a climate in which many young Englishmen of character, and some of brains, were ready to devote their lives to one aspect or another of imperial administration. These were Kipling's young men; they were the young men whose quality—particularly shewn in their power to win the sympathy and confidence of primitive races—was praised by Cromer. At home their elders campaigned, without much obvious success, for Imperial Federation and, later, for tariff reform. The ultimate aim of Empire became increasingly obscure. When formulated it might still involve independence, or at least local self-government. But such objectives were seen as a long way off; the men on the spot neither visualized nor desired them. They were caught up in day-to-day administration and had little time or imagination to spare for distant ideals.

Meanwhile, as missionary zeal and optimism abated, the methods of the administrators became increasingly 'exclusive', their social attitudes increasinglyrigid. Standards of administration improved; but this improvement itself tended to increase the gulf between the rulers and their more educated subjects. A certain aloofness was thought necessary to maintain firm and impartial government; it was in any case congenial to English reserve and pride of race. Dilke had noted in *Greater Britain* that, in contrast with French practice in Canada and Tahiti, this pride of race was 'an absolute bar to intermarriage, and even to lasting connexions with the aborigines' in America and Australia; he had mentioned the 'antipathy everywhere exhibited by the English to coloured races'. Winwood Reade had observed that the Anglo-Saxon people were 'somewhat inclined to pride of colour and prejudice of race.'

The Late Victorian bore his imperial burden with courage and discipline and sometimes with skill. But he did not bear it lightly or comfortably. Why were his mentors so insistent that he should take it up? What was the strength of their appeal?

III

Politicians and Proconsuls

---

1. ROSEBERY, RHODES AND CHAMBERLAIN

During the last fifteen years of the nineteenth century, the years of 'The New Imperialism', ministerial conduct of foreign policy virtually alternated between the Whig Rosebery (1847–1929) and the Conservative Salisbury (1830–1903). Salisbury was in power for most of these years; but Rosebery directed the Foreign Office in 1886 and from 1892 to 1894 before he became, for a brief spell, Prime Minister. Salisbury, more than any other Minister, shaped British policy during the 'Scramble for Africa'; Rosebery, aiming at a bipartisan foreign and imperial policy, was a colleague rather than a rival. Yet Salisbury, though fully alive to imperial interests, was not a publicist for Imperialist ideas in the sense that Rosebery or Chamberlain were. His approach was that of a diplomatist rather than an empire-builder; he would scarcely have said, as Rosebery did in 1881: 'Our great Empire has pulled us, so to speak, by the coat-tails, out of the European system . . . our foreign policy has become a Colonial policy. . . .' Salisbury was less concerned with the development of the Empire for its own sake than with the maintenance of British interests, throughout the world, in the face of international competition. The principles of his policy were thoroughly classic and realistic.

Rosebery's imperial vision was sharpened by travels to Australia, India and Egypt.[1] Advocating 'the closest union in sympathy, in external action and in defence' between the different

---

[1] Cf. p. 66 above.

parts of the Empire, he was a leading light of the Imperial Federation League, over which he presided for several years. He preached the League's ideals in a series of eloquent and elevated speeches. Thus he told the Leeds Chamber of Commerce in 1888 that Imperial Federation was:

'the dominant passion of my public life. Ever since I traversed those great regions which own the sway of the British crown outside these islands, I have felt that there was a cause which merited all the enthusiasm and energy that man could give to it. It is a cause for which anyone might be content to live; it is a cause for which, if needs be, anyone might be content to die.'

Curzon, though a Tory, paid tribute to the effect of these speeches at a farewell dinner before he left to take up his Viceroyalty:

'From his [Rosebery's] lips we have all of us, on many occasions, imbibed the lessons of an Imperialism, exalted but not arrogant, fearless but not rash, an Imperialism which is every day becoming less and less the creed of a party and more and more the faith of a nation.'

Contemporaries noted the contrast between Rosebery's external policies, which seemed Tory, and his concern for domestic progress, which was Radical—or at least Whig. There was something both patrician and dilettante in his attitude to party politics. At the end of his life he confessed in private conversation that he would have done better to follow Disraeli, who had fascinated him as a young man. After he left office he developed a philosophy of efficiency—implying 'the rule of the fittest'— which was hardly in the British Liberal tradition. The mainspring of his Imperialism seems to have been throughout a romantic and traditional patriotism of a type that most people would associate with Toryism rather than Liberalism. He himself described 'sane Imperialism' as 'a larger patriotism'. He might speak to the Leeds Chamber of Commerce about the commercial advantage of imperial union. But that was not the aspect of Empire that moved him. As he said on another occasion: 'Empires founded on trade alone must irresistibly crumble.' He had a strong sense of history. His imagination was stirred by the grandeur of the imperial idea, by the beneficent vistas of Anglo-Saxon expansion, stretching both into the past and into the future.

It is not very easy to distinguish Rosebery's Liberal Imperialism from any other form of Imperialism. He was careful to contrast it with 'wild cat' Imperialism and to stress that 'Empire does not live by the sword'; but there was nothing purely Liberal in that. In practice he was ready to support strong action when it seemed necessary—and did so in the case of Egypt, Afghanistan and Uganda. In 1893, when he spoke of 'pegging out claims' for the future, he suggested that imperial expansion ought not to be limited by present needs; his attitude provoked the comment from Gladstone that he 'was imbued with the spirit of territorial Grab'. At an election speech in the Albert Hall in 1895 he defined Liberal Imperialism as 'first, the maintenance of the Empire; secondly, the opening of new spaces for our surplus populations; thirdly, the suppression of the slave trade; fourthly the development of our commerce, which so often needs it.' A Tory might have put the emphasis a shade differently, but could cheerfully have subscribed to this programme. The note of 'Leadership' may be missing; but Rosebery supplied it in other speeches.

If there was anything specifically Liberal, or Whig, in Rosebery's Imperialism it lay perhaps in his readiness to contemplate the sharing of power and privileges with the colonies inside an imperial federation, and in his notion of the benefits to humanity from exporting British principles of government. '. . . The Empire that is sacred to me' he said in 1898, 'is sacred for this reason, that I believe it to be the noblest example yet known to mankind of free, adaptable, just government. . . .' He seems to have taken Chatham as his model, as well as his study; in 1899 he declared him 'the first Liberal Imperialist'. If he were still living he might have claimed Churchill as the last.

Much of Rosebery's language about the Empire, for all its sincerity and eloquence, seems strained or sentimental today. But it had imagination and sweep and, on at least one occasion, a touch of prophecy. 'We do not know what our fate may be' he told a Social Science Congress at Glasgow as a young man of 27. 'We have no right, perhaps, to hope that we may be an exception to the rule by which nations have their period of growth, and of grandeur, and of decay. It may be that all we most esteem may fade away like the glories of Babylon. But if we have done our duty well . . . our country . . . may be remembered, not ungratefully, as the mother of great commonwealths and peaceful empires that shall perpetuate the best qualities of the race.'

Rhodes (1853–1902) was inevitably nicknamed 'The Colossus'. His ambitions were on an even larger scale than his achievements. His career recalled the dreams of Raleigh, as well as the actions of Clive; but Raleigh's aims in the New World seem modest in comparison with Rhodes' vision. Since his youth his ruling passion had been the extension of the British Empire. Between 1877 (when he was 24) and 1893 he made a series of wills with the object of advancing the Empire's interests throughout the world. It was in the will of 1877 that he first earmarked his estate for the formation of a Secret Society that would extend British rule and promote British emigration. He envisaged 'the occupation by British settlers of the entire Continent of Africa, the Holy Land, the valley of the Euphrates, the Islands of Cyprus and Candia, the whole of South America, the islands of the Pacific not heretofore possessed by Great Britain, the whole of the Malay Archipelago, the seaboard of China and Japan, the ultimate recovery of the United States of America as an integral part of the British Empire, the consolidation of the whole Empire, the inauguration of a system of Colonial Representation in the Imperial Parliament which may tend to weld together the disjointed members of the Empire, and finally the foundation of so great a power as to hereafter render wars impossible and promote the best interests of humanity.'

The dream never disappeared, though its details became less fantastic and the idea of a Secret Society, organized on Jesuit lines, was ultimately superseded, for practical purposes, by the Rhodes Scholarships scheme. 'My ruling purpose is the extension of the British Empire. . . .'; 'the highest object has been to me the greatness of my country'; 'if there be a God, I think that what he would like me to do is to paint as much of Africa British-red as possible and to do what I can elsewhere to promote the unity and extend the influence of the English-speaking race'. Wealth was only a means to these ends.

No other Late Victorian Imperialist, of power or influence, had such bold aims. There is a certain parallel between Rhodes' career and that of Sir George Goldie (1846–1925), another Imperialist man of business whose basic inspiration was not commercial. Goldie, who devoted the last twenty-three years of the century to establishing British control over the trade of the Niger basin, took Rajah Brooke of Sarawak as his hero. In later life, he told Lady Gerald Wellesley, in language very reminiscent of Rhodes: 'All achievement begins with a dream. My dream, as a child, was to colour the map red.' But Goldie's field of operations was more modest and he made much less of a public impact. He is the only contemporary whose career and driving force were at all comparable with those of 'The Colossus'. Rhodes was too audacious to be really characteristic of his time; Goldie seems a more typical figure because his audacity was more restrained.

The son of a clergyman, Rhodes believed that race was taking the place of religion as a cause of strife; Imperialism gave him an outlet for his frustrated religious sense. The British[1] race was the best in the world, the most likely to promote Justice, Liberty and Peace; hence it was best that it should rule as widely as possible. If God existed, that is what He must have intended; if not, the vision was justified by a reading of the theory of Evolution. (Rhodes had imbibed W. Reade's evolutionary ideas. He once remarked on the impression that *The Martyrdom of Man* had made upon him.) The depth of feeling and tenacity of purpose which this creed evoked in Rhodes were more impressive than its intellectual basis. The shadowy ideas of Race and Evolution were summoned to justify an ideal of universal British ascendancy, which seems to have satisfied a quasi-religious craving for absolute good.

Not that Rhodes limited his vision to the success of 'the best

---

[1] W. T. Stead defined Rhodes' idea as: '. . . English-speaking man, whether British, American, Australian, or South African.' He recorded that, in his later years, Rhodes 'expressed to me his unhesitating readiness to accept the reunion of the race under the Stars and Stripes if it could not be obtained in any other way.'

people in the world'. His hopes for a red-painted globe do not seem to have involved the extermination or suppression of other races. He was neither logical enough, nor unpractical and inhuman enough, to push his theories to ruthless extremes. In practice he respected, and tried to cooperate with, the Boers as Prime Minister of Cape Colony before the Jameson Raid. He was no more far-seeing than most of his contemporaries with regard to the 'native problem' and was certainly not over-scrupulous of native rights. But, although he tended to regard the Africans as children, he said that, potentially, he did not believe them to be 'different from ourselves' and he wanted them to be trained and educated. He advocated equal rights in South Africa for every civilized man: 'What is a civilized man: A man, whether white or black, who has sufficient education to write his name, has some property or works, in fact is not a loafer.'[1]

In Rhodes' mind global British supremacy—and this was its supreme justification—would 'render wars impossible'. The world of diverse races would eventually be united under an English-speaking peace. He designed some Rhodes Scholarships for students of German birth because he thought that 'a good understanding between England, Germany, and the U.S.A. will secure the peace of the world'. In August 1891 he wrote to W. T. Stead of his hope that the name of Rhodesia 'may convey the discovery of an idea which ultimately led to the cessation of all wars and one language throughout the world. . . .' At once grand and naïve, the idea was like its author. Widespread British settlement was to leaven and shape the mass; the leadership of one race was to bring unity to mankind. As wealth was a means to the triumph of Race, so Race was a means to the triumph of Peace.

After Rosebery's rather ethereal visions, and Rhodes' colossal dreams, one expects to find something down-to-earth and matter-of-fact in Chamberlain's Imperialism. His approach to what he called 'the most inspiring idea that has ever entered into the minds of British statesmen' was in fact equally passionate and

[1] These quotations are from the biography of Rhodes by Lockhart and Woodhouse.

almost equally romantic. But his ideas were conceived in a more detailed and practical—and hence more demanding—form. He more nearly achieved success, and failed more definitely, than either Rosebery or Rhodes.

Joseph Chamberlain (1836–1914) was a relatively late convert to Imperialism. The early part of his career had been devoted to municipal improvement and, more widely, to domestic reform. He did not enter Parliament till 1876 and first held office, in 1880, as President of the Board of Trade. Like the rest of the Liberal Party he opposed, in the 'seventies, the policies of the Disraeli Government. The Afghan War seemed to him 'the natural consequence of Jingoism, Imperialism, 'British interests' and all the other phrasing of the mountebank government'.

But Chamberlain had never sympathized with doctrines of 'peace at any price'. He was too masterful and active by temperament to share the Little Englanders' approach towards foreign affairs. In external policy the bent of his Liberalism was Palmerstonian. He said in the House of Commons in 1878: 'I hold that great nations have duties and responsibilities like individuals, and there are times in which they are bound to fight not for selfish British interests, but for great causes which are in danger or great principles which are imperilled, in order to succour the oppressed and do justice to the weak'. (Palmerston, of course, had no contempt for British interests, but was able to identify them with 'great principles' and to pursue both at the same time.) In 1882 Chamberlain enlarged on this theme: 'I have always thought that a great nation like an individual had duties and responsibilities to its neighbours, and that it could not wrap itself up in a policy of selfish isolation and say that nothing concerned it unless its material interests were directly attacked. . . .'

Like most Englishmen at the time, whether Liberal or Conservative, Chamberlain believed in a continued British presence in India; in 1877 he spoke of India's happiness lying 'in the continued security of our rule.' But it was not until the early 'eighties that he began to favour a really positive and expansive attitude in imperial affairs. He supported intervention in Egypt in 1882, while proposing to 'leave Egypt to the Egyptians' once institutions had been established to guarantee their liberties and to administer justice. His patriotism was whetted by the French and German colonial expansion of these years; he particularly resented the German occupation of the Cameroons in 1884. At the same time the influence of Dilke, with whom he was closely associated in politics, and of Seeley (the *Expansion of England* was published in 1883) stimulated him to think about the desirability of closer imperial union. Ireland underlined the importance and urgency of the question. Never a supporter of Irish separatism he resigned from the Liberal Government on this issue in 1886 and wrote to a fellow M.P.: 'The hope—it may be only a distant one, but it has infinite attractions—of drawing more closely together the great dependencies of the British Crown and welding them into a mighty and harmonious Empire rests on the determination to resist in their inception all separatist tendencies. . . .'[1] In this respect Chamberlain differed from Rhodes, who believed that union in imperial matters should be balanced by effective local Home Rule.

Henceforward the cause of imperial unity was to dominate Chamberlain's thought and life. In Toronto, in 1887, he referred to 'the greatnesss and importance of the destiny which is reserved for the Anglo-Saxon race—for that proud, persistent, self-asserting and resolute stock, that no change of climate or condition can alter, and which is infallibly destined to be the predominant force in the future history and civilization of the world'. On his return to England he said at the Devonshire Club: 'I am willing to submit to the charge of being a sentimentalist when I say that I will never willingly admit of any policy that will tend to weaken the ties between the different branches of the Anglo-Saxon race which form the British Empire and the vast dominion of the Queen.'

In his Devonshire Club speech Chamberlain also stressed the supposed commercial advantages of Empire: 'Experience teaches us that trade follows the flag.' This was a motive that had strongly

---

[1] Quoted from *The Times* in Strauss: *J. Chamberlain and the Theory of Imperialism:* p. 50.

influenced the French colonial revival[1] and it was one to which Chamberlain was to give much publicity. But a study of his speeches and career suggests that, although he regarded trade as an important prize and bond of Empire, the basic reasons for his Imperialism were less immune from the charge of 'sentimentalism'. The 'Economic Motive' weighed with him more than with many contemporary British imperialists: at the Board of Trade he had become concerned about the effects of foreign tariffs on British commerce. Arguments of this kind provided a hard-headed justification for his dreams. But other factors—perhaps chiefly a rarefied form of the 'Aggressive Motive'—came first.

Greater unity within the Empire of British stock was Chamberlain's fundamental aim. In 1896 he quoted lines from Tennyson which expressed his almost mystical devotion to this ideal:

> *Britain's myriad voices call,*
> *Sons, be welded each and all,*
> *Into one Imperial whole,*
> *One with Britain, heart and soul!*
> *One life, one flag, one fleet, one Throne!*

There was, of course, a racial tinge to this devotion. He was proud of being called 'the apostle of the Anglo-Saxon race', though he claimed not to despise other races. Advocating a German-English-American understanding at Leicester in 1899 he noted that 'the main character of the Teutonic race differs very slightly from the character of the Anglo-Saxon'.

But the same qualities of adventure and enterprise, which had carried the Anglo-Saxon race to its settlements overseas, should be turned, he thought, to the benefit of the dependent Empire. If he favoured imperial expansion in the 'backward' parts of the world, it was not only for commercial reasons or because he wanted to forestall foreign competitors. It was also because he believed that Anglo-Saxon capacity for leadership imposed a duty to make the rough places plain. In 1893 he said in the House of Commons: 'We have secured for Uganda the *pax Britannica* which has been

[1] pp. 28–30 above.

so beneficial in India.' In 1889 he had visited Egypt and become convinced of the value of British administration there. Like Rosebery he thought that the British were exceptionally successful in securing the 'general goodwill' of subject races. He told the Royal Colonial Institute, in 1897, that, in the dependent colonies, 'the sense of possession has given place to a different sentiment— the sense of obligation'; British rule could only be justified 'if we can shew that it adds to the happiness and prosperity of the people. . . .' He had no doubt that it measured up to this standard. There might be imperfections; but British rule had brought with it security and material improvement; the civilizing task was providing 'scope for the exercise of those faculties and qualities which have made of us a great governing race'.

The emphasis in Chamberlain's speeches about the dependent Empire is on security, order and prosperity. The note of assimilation is seldom sounded, except when he refers to the need to spread Christianity and to redeem from superstition. He says little or nothing about the ultimate future of the subject races. No doubt he assumed that, though the work of civilization might be completed one day, it would take longer than he could foresee; there was little danger of the British running out of fields where they could exercise their talent for governing.

In 1895 Chamberlain went to the Colonial Office, which he headed for eight years. A Colonial Secretary of exceptional power, drive and ability he made a great impact on the methods of colonial administration and, having greater authority over the Treasury than his predecessors, gave a new impetus to colonial development. Although he was keener on expansion than Ministers in the 'eighties and was all for a firm line with the French over the partition of West Africa, the only substantial additions made to the Empire during his period in office were the Sudan (re-conquered for strategic reasons) and Ashanti. The greater part of his time as Colonial Secretary was, of course, over-shadowed by the Boer War and its uneasy prelude. Anxious as he was to secure British supremacy in South Africa, he was far from eager in his approach to the war and tried to avoid it. Once it had started, however, he was determined that it should be won and turned to advantage—that the spirit of imperial unity which it had aroused should not be allowed to die.

When Chamberlain left the Colonial Office in 1903, it was in order to devote himself, as a 'missionary of Empire', to the cause of tariff reform. In spite of his Free Trade upbringing, he had gradually come to believe that only tariff reform could hold the Empire of British stock together. He was obsessed with the idea that the sands were running out and that unity must be forged before it was too late. If the colonies were allowed to drift apart England would sink to the status of a fifth-rate power. In this spirit he said in Johannesburg in 1903: 'The day of small kingdoms with their petty jealousies has passed. The future is with the great empires and there is no greater empire than the British Empire. Am I not justified in the hope that there will be none more united?'

'The character of the individual,' he said at Bingley Hall in 1906, 'depends upon the greatness of the ideas upon which he rests, and the character of a nation is the same. The moral grandeur of a nation depends upon its being sometimes able to forget itself, sometimes able to think of the future of the race for which it stands. England without an Empire! Can you conceive it? England in that case would not be the England we love.'

That was Chamberlain's last speech. Two days later he had the stroke which crippled him until his death. The sort of unity which he had envisaged for the Empire was to remain a dream. Perhaps the dream was too narrow, or perhaps it was too wide; or perhaps, as one Imperialist thought, it was the fault of the British political system. Writing to Lady Edward Cecil in May, 1903, Milner gave vent to a private pessimism:

'Joe is an extraordinary man—quite absolutely on the big lines. Under a different system, he really might federate the Empire effectively and live in history with the Richelieus. . . . He is swayed by big permanent ideas. . . . Still, even Joe can make nothing great with this *system*, and what do you expect of lesser men?'[1]

---

[1] Quoted in Amery's *Chamberlain:* p. 342.

2. Cromer, Milner and Curzon

Rhodes and Chamberlain were remarkable and dynamic men, who had a great influence on their times. But British Imperialism at the turn of the century was perhaps best epitomized in the careers and attitudes of Lords Cromer, Milner and Curzon: the most powerful and the most splendid of the Proconsuls. They had much in common. All three were able and high-minded administrators. They were articulate and cultivated. They were not assimilators, but they had a real concern for the welfare of their subjects. They were autocrats who came early to power and found in the service of the Empire an opportunity for personal government rarely given to British public servants. In some other respects they differed, though less significantly.

Cromer (1841–1917) was a Whig and a Free Trader with, as a member of the Baring family, an inherited respect for finance. At one time he thought of standing for parliament in the Liberal interest. He had served in India before being appointed, at the age of 42, British Agent and Consul-General in Egypt. With this unassuming title he virtually governed Egypt for 24 years, from 1883 to 1907. Known in India as the 'vice-Viceroy' and in Egypt as 'over-Baring', he impressed those who met him with his stolid self-reliance. Never a seeker of popularity himself he was quite ready to admit that the British were not popular in Egypt, though he thought that this want of sympathy was 'mitigated by the respect due to superior talents, and by the benefits which have accrued to the population from British interference'. Like many other British administrators he fortified himself against the hostility of the more advanced classes by the thought of his efforts on behalf of the peasants. In *Modern Egypt* he expressed the hope (though he was clear-sighted enough to realize that it was an uncertain one) that the Egyptian *fellaheen* might 'remember with some feeling akin to gratitude that it was the Anglo-Saxon race who first delivered them from the thraldom of their oppressors. . . .'

Cromer was an Imperialist of the 'Leader' type. Conscious of the 'superior talents' of the Anglo-Saxon race, he believed they could provide Egypt with practical benefits: a sound accounting system, irrigation, law, freedom from tyranny. These were the blessings that, in India, they had poured 'on the heads of the ryots of Bengal and Madras'. He accepted that 'the new generation of Egyptians has to be persuaded or forced into imbibing the true spirit of Western civilization'; but he felt more confident of the material, than of the moral, advantages of British rule. 'The material benefits derived from Europeanization are unquestionably great, but as regards the ultimate effect on public and private morality the future is altogether uncertain. European civilization destroys one religion without substituting another in its place. . . . This question can only be answered by generations which are now unborn.' Although not opposed to the idea of assimilation, he was sceptical about the power of modern empires to assimilate. He attached great importance to the establishment of a School of Oriental Studies in England and, if he could have obtained Moslem support, would have preferred to revive Egyptian education by creating an indigenous system, not one on the European model. That a Whig should have come to this point illustrates the change in the temper of British Imperialism since the days of Macaulay.

When he first came to Egypt Cromer was sympathetic to the idea of British withdrawal. He continued to regard Egyptian autonomy as the eventual aim, but soon decided that it could not be an early one. He had become obsessed with the work which, in his opinion, needed doing first; besides, as he hinted in *Modern Egypt*, Egypt was strategically too important to be left to 'stew in its own juice'. In *Ancient and Modern Imperialism* he suggested that the Roman Imperialist, like his modern French, Russian, German and Italian counterparts, would have had no difficulty in answering the question: *Quo Vadis?* Each of them would reply that his intention was 'to civilize his alien subjects, but in no way to relax his hold over them'. The English Imperialist, on the other hand, would find the question harder, because he was struggling after two ideals which were apt to be mutually destructive: good government and self-government. The Whig in Cromer still looked forward to eventual self-government;

meanwhile he allowed the administrator's concern with 'good government' to prevail. In India he was inclined to think that, because of the country's lack of homogeneity, even the ultimate aim should not be independence so much as local government under remote British control. For the present the 'foundation-stone of Indian reform must be the steadfast maintenance of British supremacy'.

Cromer's success in restoring Egyptian finances, his care for the welfare of the peasantry, were out-weighed, in the minds of educated Egyptians, by the cold sense of superiority—which he must personally have epitomized—of their British rulers. But Cromer never expected the occupation of Egypt to benefit Great Britain, except in the strategic sense of excluding other powers, or from the general point of view of maintaining prosperity and trade. Did it, in the end, benefit Egypt? The answer must lie, not in the feelings of Egyptians about Great Britain, but in the subsequent development of Egypt herself. Her attainment of genuine independence, for the first time in centuries, is a fact which can no doubt be interpreted in different ways. But it is not to Cromer's discredit.

Milner (1854–1925) served under Cromer in Egypt before becoming British High Commissioner in South Africa, in 1897, at the age of 43. A streak of 'Germanic thoroughness' in his make-up is often traced to his German grandmother and partly German education. Grave, sensitive and tense, he was more of a professional Imperialist than his former chief. He wrote in 1913 that his public activities had been 'dominated by a single desire—that of working for the integrity and consolidation of the British Empire'. His interest in the Empire went back to his days at Oxford. At a farewell dinner before he went out to take up his South African appointment he said '. . . there is one question upon which I have never been able to see the other side, and that is precisely this question of Imperial Unity'; to promote it he became a firm advocate of Tariff Reform. There was a religious fervour in Milner's Imperialism, as there was in that of Rhodes and Kipling. 'Imperialism as a political doctrine', he wrote in his Introduction

F   81 to *The Nation and the Empire*, 'has often been represented as something tawdry and superficial. In reality it has all the depth and comprehensiveness of a religious faith. . . . It is a question of preserving the unity of a great race, of enabling it, by maintaining that unity, to develop freely on its own lines, and to continue to fulfil its distinctive mission in the world.'

Milner was a brilliant administrator, impatient of politics, qualifications and delays, who had no special love of democracy and would refer to 'that mob at Westminster'. His views were clear, definite and co-ordinated; but his intense single-mindedness was a source of weakness as well as of strength. His object in South Africa was to create a united and outward-looking society under British supremacy. Having this object firmly in mind he helped to make the Boer War inevitable. But his enlightened efforts of reconstruction after the War were frustrated, except on the material plane, by the concessions to the Boers made by the Liberal Party when it came to power in 1906. It is difficult to judge now whether his policy of 'thorough' could ever have succeeded. Even if it could, it must have been incomplete since, like most of his contemporaries, Milner under-estimated the 'native factor' in South Africa. His views on the Negro population seem to have been something like those of Rhodes: 'civilization', not colour, should be the criterion for enjoyment of full civic rights.

With all his sense of British superiority Cromer looked at Egyptian problems from an Egyptian angle—and with a detached understanding of the Egyptian point of view. Milner shewed the same kind of understanding in his able and attractive book on *England in Egypt*. But, in South Africa, his basic concern was imperial, rather than local: he wanted to prevent 'the weakest link in the imperial chain' from snapping. He was not an aggressive Jingo, but he was determined to hold the Empire together. He told the Manchester Conservative Club in 1906:

'Empire and Imperialism are words which lend themselves to much misuse. It is only when stripped of tawdry accessories that the ideas which they imperfectly express can be seen in their real greatness. Our object is not domination or aggrandisement. It is consolidation and security. We envy and antagonize no other nation. But we wish the kindred peoples under the British flag to remain one united family for ever'.

Milner's chief interest lay in imperial unity between the settlements of British stock. The racial bond was what counted most with him; he told Rhodes, when appointed a Trustee of his will, that he was 'in complete sympathy with your broad ambitions for the race'. With regard to the dependent Empire he felt the responsibilities of the 'Leader' type of Imperialist, the need to be paternal, though not oppressive, towards the coloured races. Like Cromer he looked forward to some kind of autonomy in India; the capacities of the Indians for self-government must be brought out; but he assumed that progress would be slow. In *England in Egypt* (1892) he took a cautiously liberal line: 'I do not believe that the indefinite continuance of British control in its present form is essential to the ultimate welfare of Egypt. I see great improvement in the self-governing capacity of its inhabitants and I look forward to still greater improvements in the same direction.' That he was not a real assimilator, in spite of the general tendency of his South African policy, appears in a passage in the Introduction to *The Nation and the Empire* where he says that he does not advocate 'anglicization' of the non-British races of the Empire such as the French Canadians or the Boers.

Curzon (1859–1925), a Tory Imperialist since his youth, became Viceroy of India at the age of 39. He had already succumbed to the glamour of the East. Before leaving London he said that he loved 'India, its people, its history, its government, the absorbing mysteries of its civilization and its life'. Throughout his life he remembered, almost with passion, his oriental travels as a young man. He dedicated his book on *Persia and the Persian Question*, published in 1892, to:

THE OFFICIALS, CIVIL AND MILITARY, IN INDIA
WHOSE HANDS UPHOLD
THE NOBLEST FABRIC YET REARED
BY THE GENIUS OF A CONQUERING NATION
I DEDICATE THIS WORK

POLITICIANS AND PROCONSULS

THE UNWORTHY TRIBUTE OF THE PEN TO A CAUSE
WHICH BY JUSTICE OR WITH THE SWORD
IT IS THEIR HIGH MISSION TO DEFEND
BUT WHOSE ULTIMATE SAFEGUARD IS THE SPIRIT OF THE
BRITISH PEOPLE.

In the Introduction to this work he claimed:

'The future of Great Britain . . . will be decided, not in Europe, not even upon the seas and oceans which are swept by her flag, or in the Greater Britain that has been called into existence by her offspring, but in the continent whence our emigrant stock first came, and to which as conquerors their descendants have returned. Without India the British Empire could not exist. The possession of India is the inalienable badge of sovereignty in the eastern hemisphere . . .'

Milner's imagination was caught by a vision of the family of British peoples encircling the globe. Curzon's more romantic and more magnificent taste was gratified by the idea of despotic, though beneficent, sway over oriental peoples. In this, and in his delight in colourful power politics, he resembled Disraeli. He resembled him, too, in the tendency towards 'assimilation in reverse' shewn in his attitude towards his high office, in his care for the relics of the Indian past ('Indian art will never be revived by borrowing foreign ideals, but only by fidelity to its own') and in his discouragement of Indian notables from wearing European dress. Like Cromer he had a paternal concern for the welfare of the peasantry; he also set his hand to reorganize Indian primary education, on the principle that, under the 'cold breath of Macaulay's rhetoric', vernacular education had been neglected. When it came to Higher Education, however, he held that, though there might have been 'a too slavish imitation of English models', the policy based on Macaulay's Minute of providing a European, rather than an Asiatic, education was not only irreversible, but on the whole justified by results.[1]

In spite of his respect for Indian traditions and prejudices

---

[1] For an interesting light on Curzon's educational policy. See *High Noon of Empire.* by Michael Edwardes (1965).

Curzon had the usual Imperialist sense of British moral superiority and capacity to rule. He was struck by 'the enormous administrative ability of the English race' and claimed that efficiency 'has been the gospel, the key note of our administration'. His farewell message before leaving India was:

'. . . To feel that somewhere among these millions you have left a little justice or happiness or prosperity, a sense of manliness or moral dignity, a spring of patriotism, a dawn of intellectual enlightenment, or a stirring of duty where it did not exist before— that is enough, that is the Englishman's justification in India.'

A spring of patriotism? The phrase recalls Lord Dufferin's report on Egypt in February, 1883, when he had written of implanting 'those instincts of patriotism and freedom which it has been our boast to foster in every country where we have set our foot.' As Viceroy of India Dufferin extended a cautious patronage to the new, and at first respectful, National Congress. Curzon preferred the patriotism of Indian Princes to the patriotism of nationalist politicians. His period as Viceroy (from 1899 to 1905) in some ways marked the apogee of the Indian Empire; he had certainly no wish to preside over its dissolution. When he spoke of 'patriotism' he did not mean an exclusively Indian sentiment; any desire for freedom from British rule would have struck him as distinctly *un*-patriotic. He had in mind what he told the Convocation of Calcutta University in 1902: 'Out of this intermingling of the East and West, a new patriotism, and a more refined and cosmopolitan sense of nationality, are emerging. It is one in which the Englishman may share with the Indian, for he has helped to create it, and in which the Indian may share with the Englishman, since it is their common glory. . . . Let the Englishman and the Indian accept the consecration of a union that is so mysterious as to have in it something of the divine. . . .' Politically speaking the union, if it ever existed, proved too mysterious to last. But the last word could yet be Curzon's. Three years later he told the same audience: 'As nationality is larger than race, so is Empire larger than nationality. . . . Race weakens and gets overlaid in the passage of time and gives place to broader conceptions.'

IV

Prophets

'The New Imperialism' depended upon the pen, at least as much as upon the ledger and the sword. The writings of Dilke, Froude and Seeley were particularly influential in opening the eyes of their contemporaries to the potentialities of Empire.

Sir Charles Wentworth Dilke, second Baronet (1843–1911), a rising Liberal-Radical politician until in 1885 he became involved in a famous adultery scandal, made a tour of English-speaking countries (America, Polynesia, Australia and India) in 1866–7, as a young man of 23. He published the record of this tour under the striking title of *Greater Britain* in 1868. The work had an extraordinary success, attaining a fourth edition in 1869. J. S. Mill, who had at that time never met Dilke, wrote to congratulate him: 'It is long since any book connected with practical politics has been published on which I build such high hopes of the future usefulness and distinction of the writer, shewing, as it does, that he not only possesses a most unusual amount of real knowledge on many of the principal questions of the future, but a mind strongly predisposed to what are (at least in my opinion) the most advanced and enlightened views of them.' It is interesting that this progressive sage, although critical of Dilke's emphasis on the influence of race and climate on national character, should not have been put off the book by its repeated theme of Anglo-Saxon supremacy. The two men continued to correspond on many topics, including colonial policy.

In his travels Dilke 'followed England round the world' and found that 'in essentials the race was always one'; he took with him a conception of 'the grandeur of our race, already girdling the earth, which it is destined, perhaps, eventually to overspread'. At one point he refers to a growing view in England that 'love of mankind must in time replace love of race'; but it was race, more than humanity, that kindled his own imagination. He stresses continually, without apparent disapproval, English racial pride. He noted that 'The Anglo-Saxon is the only extirpating race on earth' and accepts the gradual extinction of inferior races (when, like some Red Indian tribes, really debased) as a law of nature. His interest begins with the settlements of British stock, but he extends it to the tropical Empire, where he observes the interplay of 'dearer' and 'cheaper' races. He sees 'the English horde, ever pushing with burning energy towards the setting sun' and carrying Saxon institutions and the English tongue with them. He assumes that China will eventually fall to the English horde, together with Chile, Peru, Japan and the African table lands. 'The abstract injustice of annexation cannot be said to exist in the cases of Afghanistan and Abyssinia, as the sentiment of nationality clearly has no existence there and as the worst possible form of British government is better for the mass of the people than the best conceivable rule of an Abyssinian chief'.

Dilke regarded the U.S.A. as, basically, English. Although he feared the effects of Irish hostility, he was confident that the English mould was forming America, which consequently offered the 'English race the moral directorship of the globe, by ruling mankind through Saxon institutions and the English tongue'. He would prefer Great Britain to equal the U.S.A. in power and he thought that the possession of India made this possible. But he was not alarmed by the prospect that the Americans might come to predominate. In the authentic strain of Whig/Liberal expansion he wrote that the main thing was to keep 'English laws and principles of government' for the freedom of mankind.

In spite of his excessive claims for the Anglo-Saxon race (*Great Britain* was, of course, a young man's book), Dilke was a Liberal and a Free Trader who was not interested in retaining colonies

for reasons of prestige. He was ready to contemplate independence for Australia, though he seems to have hoped for the
maintenance of some connection, if only because the existence of
the Empire helped to raise Great Britain above provincialism.
('That which raises us above the provincialism of little England is
our citizenship of the greater Saxondom which includes all that is
best and wisest in the world.') He did not think that separation
would, in the case of Australia, have an adverse effect on British
trade. He was less certain of this in the case of India; but the
uncertainty seems to have weighed less with him than the fear that
British withdrawal would lay India open either to anarchy or to
Russian despotism. He leaves it an open question 'whether
we are ever to leave India or whether we are to remain there till
the end of time'. Meanwhile he is clear that the Indian races must
be educated for freedom. He is in favour of more opportunities
for Indians in the government; points out that the Chinese or the
Negro can in some cases outwork the white man; disapproves of
too much colour bar or of discourtesy towards 'inferior races'. He
criticizes various aspects of British behaviour in India. One
criticism, of 'our somewhat blind love of "progress",' is sympto-
matic of the movement away from assimilation. But he compares
favourably the imperial record of the British with that of the
contemporary Dutch, taking it for granted that the British were
not out to exploit their tropical dependencies for exploitation's
sake. In general his attitude is less aggressive than his language
would sometimes suggest; there is a relaxed and happy inevitabi-
lity about his dreams of Anglo-Saxon triumph.

Over twenty years later Dilke followed up *Greater Britain*
with a more sober and documentary work, *Problems of Greater
Britain*, which also had a wide sale. In this book he describes the
earlier one as 'wholly out of date'. He still strikes the same note of
Anglo-Saxon racial supremacy; still hopes for a balance between
the U.S.A. and Great Britain (now to be achieved by the growth
of Canada and Australia); yet still regards the American and
British peoples as 'essentially one'. He has the insight to antici-
pate a struggle between the Anglo-Saxons and the Russians and to
worry about imperial defence. He likes the idea of Imperial

Federation, but knows that it cannot be forced. Exaggerating the advantage in power accruing to Great Britain from a self-governing Empire, he expects France and Germany to seem pygmies by comparison in a century's time.

Perhaps the main change in tone between the two books is a more critical attitude towards tropical expansion in *Problems of Greater Britain*. In this later work Dilke argues that, up till about 1884, both parties did their best to avoid territorial expansion:

'Lord Palmerston had declined such gifts as firmly as had Mr. Disraeli or Mr. Gladstone. The semi-annexation of Cyprus was defended solely upon military grounds. In the case of Fiji the annexation had been forced upon us . . . by the impossibility of putting down ruffianism in any other way. . . . A necessary change of policy followed on the discovery that Germany and France appeared to intend to lay hands between them upon almost all those territories in the globe which did not belong to the European races.' He refers to the gospel preached (how mildly!) by M. Leroy-Beaulieu and suggests that 'England could not well but follow the lead given'. But: 'It is nevertheless difficult to restrain a feeling of regret that in African partition we have been forced to follow France and Germany upon a path which we had in former times deliberately abandoned'. Nothing is now heard about annexing Afghanistan and Abyssinia.

Dilke was a clever and penetrating man, whose enthusiasms were firm and lasting, but not always very consistent with each other. Although he told the Chelsea electors in 1868 that 'Our true alliance is not with the Latin peoples . . .', he was, like Kipling, a great Francophile, particularly after the fall of the Second Empire. His belief in the Anglo-Saxon race did not prevent him from being a strong supporter of native rights. He worked for the Congo Reform Association and the Aborigines Protection Society and—unlike most Liberals of his time—was wary of allowing the Boers too free a hand in their dealings with the African population. His interest in imperial defence was lifelong (he published a book on it in 1898); but he was only occasionally an expansive Imperialist. In 1875 he wrote: 'I am as great a Jingo in Central Asia as I am a scuttler in South Africa'. He supported the decision of the Gladstone Government to withdraw from the Sudan in 1884; he opposed the retention of Uganda a decade later; and he observed of the Prince of Wales:

'The Prince is, of course, in fact, a strong Conservative, and a still stronger Jingo, really agreeing in the Queen's politics, and wanting to take everything everywhere in the world. . . .'[1]

A Liberal-Radical Imperialist could hardly escape a mild schizophrenia of this kind. It was at all times typical enough of British Imperialism.

J. A. Froude (1818–1894), the historian and biographer of Carlyle, was one of the first to react against the *laissez-faire* views fashionable in the 'sixties, and to assert a tighter form of patriotism. In two articles published in 1870 he pleaded for a greater expansion of state-assisted emigration to the colonies, in order to lessen the pressure at home, to improve the living conditions of the lower class, to maintain a healthy country-bred stock throughout the Empire and the strengthen 'the British Realm'. He castigated the Liberal Government's attitude of indifference to the colonies, argued that the times were not made for small states and looked forward to the 'indefinite and magnificent expansion of the English Empire'. Apart from planned emigration and the admission of colonial citizens to metropolitan honours, he had no detailed precepts to offer for imperial union. 'Healthy confederations must grow and cannot be made.' (This was also Dilke's view.) Like Disraeli, Froude was a believer in the 'sentimental values' and contemptuous of political economy as 'the sole rule of statesmanship'.

Sir J. Skelton testified to the influence of these articles in 1895: 'From this time onwards the policy of Imperial Federation—or at least of a closer connexion between the Mother Country and the Colonies—was urgently advocated by Mr. Froude. There can be no doubt that to his urgent advocacy the sounder views that now prevail are in some measure due.' According to a letter to the *Pall Mall Gazette* in 1897: 'It is meet and right that at the present hour we should not forget the man whose far sight first saw and

[1] Quoted in *Sir Charles Dilke* by Roy Jenkins: p. 144.

whose splendid genius familiarised us with the romantic idea of our country's greatness. . . . The Colonial procession on Jubilee Day is in a great measure due to the brave and patient teaching of James Anthony Froude. He first raised his voice against the measures being taken and the language being used by responsible statesmen which were indisputably designed to lead to certain and early disintegration of the Empire'.[1]

In 1870 Froude's attitude was still narrowly English. He thought it was mistaken to rely on emigration to the U.S.A., which might one day become a hostile power. In 1872 he feared that the 'Anglo-Saxon power is running to seed' in America. However, during the 'seventies, his attitude towards the U.S.A. seems to have become more like Dilke's. In 1878 he referred to the Americans as 'the people of the future'; and again: 'There, not here, is the future of the English race'. In 1881 he wrote to an American: 'I have come reluctantly to recognize that the future of the Anglo-Saxon race is with you and not with us.' Accepting the logic of this he hoped and believed 'that a time will come when there will no longer be Englishmen and Americans, but we shall be of one heart and mind, and perhaps of one name.'[2]

Froude was an impulsive man and not always a judicious one. Firmly persuaded that a nation's greatness consisted in the moral soundness (health, strength, truth, bravery, sobriety, temperance and chastity) of its human beings, he was seduced by the discovery of these qualities in the Boers and, for this and other reasons, did not make much of a success of a mission to South Africa which he undertook at Lord Carnarvon's behest. Together with most people at the time he was blind to the urgency of the 'native' problem there. His attitude to the Africans—whom he was apt to call 'Niggers'—was one of good-humoured superiority. Like Rhodes he did not think there was any absolute difference between them and the whites; but he believed that they needed a long period of training and discipline. He wrote in 1878: 'For all I know, the black race may be as good as the others when it has

---

[1] Both passages quoted in the biography of Froude by W. H. Dunn, Vol. 2: pp. 352 and 605.
[2] Dunn: *op. cit.*: p. 353.

gone through the same training. Hitherto the Negro has had no chance; he has been a slave from the beginning of history.' Nine years later he found in the West Indies 'no original or congenital difference of capacity. . . . But it does not follow that what can be done eventually can be done immediately . . . if we give the Negroes as a body the political power which we claim for ourselves, they will use it only to their own injury'. He thought the West Indian Negroes were happy under British rule and that they must not be allowed to travel Haiti's path to the bonfire of independence, savagery and decline.

I have already quoted a passage from Froude which illustrates his 'Leadership' brand of Imperialism.[1] He criticised in his journal, during his tour of the West Indies in 1887, British 'persistence in applying to conquered countries and colonies a form of self-government which can only succeed among men of our own race who are part of ourselves and of whose loyalty there can be no question; . . . Instead of trying to help our colonies, and give them advantages in belonging to us, we have given them, as we did Ireland,[2] doses of the modern *elixir vitae* political liberty, and then we wonder that they are not grateful and affectionate. The hungry belly has been fed with the East Wind, with the usual consequences.' He much admired the system of British rule in India and wrote in *The English and the West Indies* of 'those who, like most Asiatics, do not desire liberty and prosper best when they are led and guided'.

In spite of his intense patriotism Froude was not a Jingo. He was against involvement in European complications and disliked the 'glory and gunpowder' of Disraeli's Eastern policy.[3] His interest as an Imperialist lay mainly in the new world of the colonies of British stock. In 1886 he published *Oceana*, a record of travel in Australasia, which was at the same time a plea for the

---

[1] p. 62 above.

[2] A fuller study of 19th Century British Imperialism would, of course, need to do justice to the effects of the Irish question on Imperialist opinion. Cf. p. 75 above.

[3] 'The spirit of a great nation called into energy on a grand occasion is the noblest of human phenomena. The pseudo-national spirit of jingoism is the meanest and the most dangerous.' (Froude: *Lord Beaconsfield:* p. 251).

organic growth of imperial unity, for 'a "comonwealth" of Oceana held together by common blood, common interest and a common pride in the great position which unity can secure. . . .' The book sold 75,000 copies.

Sir J. R. Seeley (1834–1895), Professor of Modern History at Cambridge and author of *Ecce Homo*, was closely connected with the Imperial Federation League and a 'Liberal Unionist' in his later years. According to the *Dictionary of National Biography* his celebrated lectures, published under the title of *The Expansion of England* in July, 1883, '. . . contributed perhaps more than any other single utterance to the change of feeling respecting the relations between Great Britain and her colonies which marks the end of the nineteenth century'. At the 1884 Westminster Palace Hotel Conference, at which the Imperial Federation League was founded, a speaker proposed that one of the League's first actions should be to have the book printed and circulated in England and the colonies. It was in this work that Seeley coined the phrase about British 'absence of mind': 'There is something very characteristic in the indifference which we show towards this mighty phenomenon of the diffusion of our race and the expansion of our state. We seem, as it were, to have conquered and peopled half the world in a fit of absence of mind . . . we do not reckon our colonies as really belonging to us . . .'

The Expansion of England deals with the colonies of British settlement and with India. Written before the 'Scramble for Africa' it does not touch on the lesser tropical dependencies. It is very clearly and persuasively written and is remarkable for its moderate and sober tone. Far from ministering to Jingoism, Seeley attacks the 'bombastic' school of historians and is careful not to over-write the British achievement. One of the purposes of the lectures is to demonstrate the indispensability of history to politicians. Another is to bring out the true character of the Anglo-French wars of the eighteenth century by stressing their colonial aspect.

Apart from these more academic aims Seeley has the practical object of challenging public indifference to the Empire. He suggests that there is no point in asking 'What is the good of the colonies?' or in arguing—quite rightly, he accepts—that it is barbaric for one community to be treated as a 'possession' by another. The Colonies are, in reality, a simple extension of the English state, necessitated (unlike the first, primarily mercantile, British Empire) by pressure of population. The existing Empire need not, and must not, go the way of the first. Improved communications and the collapse of the old Mercantilist system have made a close and continuing union possible. The colonies must now really be made a part of England. Otherwise Great Britain will inevitably be overshadowed, in an age of increasingly bigger *ensembles*, by the U.S.A. and Russia.

If this last argument recalls Dilke and Froude (though Dilke criticized, in *Problems of Greater Britain*, Seeley's suggestion that Greater Britain could federate with the ease of the U.S.A.), Seeley is a good deal more restrained than either in his references to Anglo-Saxon prowess. 'The English, as such,' he observes, 'are perhaps not a race of Hellenic intelligence or genius'. The racial note is barely struck in *The Expansion of England*, except for one passage where he refers, in the fashionable language of the day, to 'the Greco-Italian Branch of the Aryan family' and another where he speaks of 'deterioration of the national type by barbaric intermixture'.

Seeley's treatment of British India is similarly cool. He points out that the British were able to conquer India not so much because of their own heroism as because it was not 'a nationality'. In spite of the value of its trade (assessed at £60 million) he thought that the possession of India was probably more of a liability than an asset to British security. Equally the benefits to India were open to question. European civilization was on the whole superior to Indian, remarkable though some of the achievements of the latter had been; but it was 'perhaps not absolutely the glorious thing we like to imagine it'. It was to be feared that it did India harm as well as good. However, there was great positive value in 'something like the *immensa majestas Romanae pacis* established among 250 millions of human beings'; it would be unthinkable to try to reverse the tide of events and to abandon India to anarchy.

KIPLING

The Expansion of England was not a plea for fresh expansion, but for the consolidation of the English state overseas. This was also the concern of Dilke and Froude. The Indian Empire was, for Seeley, an exceptional and romantic adventure, to be prolonged for the sake of the 'immense majesty of the British peace', under which Kipling was born.

2. KIPLING

Kipling (1865–1936) was younger than Dilke by twenty-two years and belonged to a different generation from Froude and Seeley. But he achieved fame as a writer in his twenties, when the nineteenth century had over a decade to run. So it is fair to count him as a Late Victorian. As to the title of Imperialist his work speaks for itself. The Empire bulks heavy both in his verse and in his prose. Apart from the Indian tales, there are the stories on South Africa, the Sudan (*Little Foxes*) and Central Africa (*A Deal in Cotton*); there is, of course, a quantity of stirring and chastising verse; there is the treatment of imperial themes in *From Sea to Sea* and *Letters of Travel;* there are also less direct references in the Roman stories (including *The Church at Antioch* in the last collection), in the stories about Westward Ho! Stalky and the Infant, and in parables like *The Mother Hive*. A great deal of the rest of Kipling's writing is unmistakably coloured by his Imperialist—or at least by his patriotic—outlook.

Kipling himself supports the view that his Imperialist message was central to his work. In a well-known passage in *Something of Myself* he says:

'Bit by bit my original notion grew into a vast, vague, conspectus—Army and Navy Stores List if you like—of the whole sweep and meaning of things and effort and origins throughout the Empire. I visualized it, as I do most ideas, in the shape of a semicircle of buildings and temples projecting into a sea of dreams.'

Patriotism and Imperialism went hand in hand: effort at the frontier and continuity at home. The Sussex stories (*Puck of Pook's Hill, Rewards and Fairies*), with their quiet colours and fresh scents, contrast pleasantly with Kipling's more strident writings; but at bottom they bear on the same theme. Kipling himself, a highly self-conscious artist, was completely aware of this. He called these stories in *Something of Myself*:

'. . . a sort of balance to, as well as a seal upon, some aspects of my 'Imperialistic' output in the past.'

There are some obvious personal explanations for this imperial bias. Because his father held posts in Indian Art Schools, Kipling's early childhood was spent in India and he returned there for a few years, to work as a journalist, at the age of seventeen. He was thus confronted, at an impressionable age, with the majesty of the Indian Empire during one of its more august and tranquil periods. His respect for those who served it coloured his views for life. In 1908 (when he was forty-three) he told a Naval Club:

'The circumstances of my early training happened to throw me among disciplined men of action—men who belonged to one or other of the Indian Services—men who were therefore accustomed to act under orders, and to live under authority, as the good of their service required. . . . I did not realize, then, what I realized later, that the men who belong to the Services . . . constitute a very small portion of our world, and do not attract much of its attention or its interest.'

Then there was the place and time of his education. Although there seems to have been nothing particularly militarist about Kipling at school, he was educated at the recently founded United Services College, Westward Ho!, where his fellow pupils were mostly officers' sons, destined to follow an Army career. In 1878, when he entered the College, Disraeli was Prime Minister. '. . . It is not to be forgotten that these susceptible years were also the years of the Russo-Turkish War, of Indian troops at Malta, and the great Jingo song.'[1]

In later life the Imperialist connection, once formed, was maintained by travels in Canada and elsewhere, by regular visits to South Africa and by association with like-minded men, such as Henley, Rhodes and Milner.

At a deeper level the influence of heredity, in forming Kipling's

---

[1] G. M. Young in the *Dictionary of National Biography*.

views, is striking. His grandfathers, who were both Methodist Ministers, bequeathed the preaching strain which is so obvious in his work. In *Something of Myself* he describes himself, in passing, as 'a political Calvinist'. It came naturally to him to see the devil abroad (the destructive power of liberalism), to warn and to exhort. Since he was not a convinced Christian, he needed a political theme on which he could moralize and which could occupy his dreams. His prose and his verse are full of Biblical allusions; he recurs, in an almost Puritanical spirit, to the virtue of clean, simple things; he dwells on the austerities of Empire, at least as much as on its pomps. *Recessional* was written in this mood. Afterwards the Rev. F. W. Macdonald, his uncle, wrote to congratulate him with the words: '. . . the thought occurred to many that the grandfathers had spoken in you.'

Another family influence, less often recalled, was the Pre-Raphaelite tradition of craftsmanship which surrounded Kipling's early years. This is clearly evident in his compressed, balanced and patterned writing. He shortened and polished his stories like a carpenter planing wood and even lovingly described the 'tools' of his trade in *Something of Myself*. Many quotations from his work would shew the value he attached to craftsmanship. Talking to the Royal College of Surgeons in 1923 he spoke of '. . . the dearly prized, because unpurchasable, acknowledgement of one's fellow-craftsmen'. In *Wireless* (from *Traffics and Discoveries*:1904) he praises a chemist for his craft: 'I conceived great respect for Apothecaries' Hall, and esteem for Mr. Cashell, a zealous craftsman who magnified his calling.' In *From Sea to Sea* he criticizes American versatility: 'No man can grasp the inwardness of an employ by the light of pure reason. . . . He must serve an apprenticeship to one craft and learn that craft all the days of his life, if he wishes to excel therein.'

Kipling's interest in craftsmanship, heightened by a journalist's curiosity and tendency to 'type' people, led him to an intense and sustained interest in the way men do their work. At the same time his moralizing side approved of work as an end in itself. He gave the title of *The Day's Work* to one of his collections of stories. He delighted in portraying not only engineers, but also the machines (ships, trains, early motor cars) they tended. A machine had its job to do, like a man; it had its own energy and its own discipline. He was apt to see and describe men, not as deserving interest in themselves, but in function of the work they did; it was natural that he should come to regard a man's work as his making and salvation. Thus in the late story *Dayspring Mishandled* he says of Castorlley, the Chaucer expert, that 'sometimes he could break from his obsession and prove how a man's work will try to save the soul of him'. One of the least vulnerable aspects of British rule in India, towards the end of the nineteenth century, was the officials' capacity for work and their sense of duty.[1] It was typical of Kipling that he should admire their efforts, and become fascinated by their expertise, without questioning their ultimate aims or seeking for justification outside the work itself.

Again, the combined instincts of the craftsman and the moralist suggested to Kipling that there was one proper way of doing everything under the sun. Traces of this attitude appear not only in the obvious pleasure he takes in penetrating professional secrets, in being 'in the know', but also in the frequency with which he reverts to the theme of making the crooked straight. He seems to have found some deep emotional satisfaction in the concept of restoring a broken human being to mental or physical wholeness, of bringing the lost or misguided back to true. No doubt this was partly because of his own experience of nervous exhaustion and mental agony; but the question had particular urgency for him because of his tendency to assume that there was one fitting path for each man or woman, depending on his birth or calling, to take. (The following stories seem to illustrate this theme, in one way or another: *In the Same Boat, The Dog Hervey, The Woman in His Life, Fairy-Kist, The Tender Achilles, Captains Courageous, The Honours of War, My Son's Wife, His Private Honour*. The last four have nothing to do with nervous or physical illness.)

Applied to politics this attitude to life imposed a Platonic

[1] Cf. Lord Dufferin, speaking at the Mansion House in 1889: 'I did not know what hard work really meant until I witnessed the unremitting and almost inconceivable severity of the grind to which our Indian civil servants . . . so zealously devote themselves.'

conception of ruling as an art, to be learned and practised by qualified people in a certain way. Kipling seems to have conceded little more place for consent in political life than in a well-run army—except insofar as the rulers, or officers, must respect the established rights of their followers. He had of course nothing but contempt for 'counting noses' and for the noise, confusion and ignorance involved in democratic processes. This distrust of Democracy was confirmed after the Liberal victory of 1906. In 1907 he wrote, after a visit to Canada: 'Meantime, the only serious enemy to the Empire, within or without, is that very Democracy which depends on the Empire for its proper comforts.'

Kipling's attitude towards Leadership was supported by an almost girlish capacity for hero-worship. Throughout his life he shewed a tendency not only to admire, but to idealize, Great Men. As a young man he may have had more sympathy for the man on the spot than for his remote superiors. But he extended his admiration to the Proconsuls (Dufferin, Milner, Curzon) as he got to know them. Although he was seldom likely to revere politicians, Joseph Chamberlain's resignation moved him to write, in 1904, of the 'simple central truth' that:

Things never yet created things—
Once on a time there was a Man.

In *Rewards and Fairies* and *A Deal in Cotton* he writes of 'Great Ones' as if, when the real thing, they know instinctively how to behave and how to recognize each other. In *From Sea to Sea* (describing a journey to Japan in 1889) he says:

'Japan is the second Oriental country which has made it impossible for a strong man to govern alone. This she has done of her own free will. India, on the other hand, has been forcibly ravished by the Secretary of State and the English M.P. Japan is luckier than India.'

Nothing is more typical of this side of Kipling than the well-known lines from *The Ballad of East and West:*

But there is neither East nor West, Border, nor Breed, nor
Birth
When two strong men stand face to face, though they come
from the ends of the earth!'

Kipling would never have subscribed to Lord Acton's dictum about power and corruption. He had a deep reverence for the loneliness, difficulty and responsibility of high place, when held by a man ready to make his own decisions. Far from corrupting the holder, it enhanced (for Kipling) his dignity and virtue. This sense of the majesty of power was an essential element in Kipling's Imperialist vision.

Any attempt to expound visions risks causing them to evaporate. Kipling was an artist and something of a mystic; he was not a trained political thinker. As a mystic he had a strong, intuitive, sense of certain values, which he embodied in his concept of Empire. As an artist he displayed the Empire—and these values —in a wide range of scenes and activities. However much its incompleteness or one-sidedness may be criticized, the vision can never be entirely destroyed because, apart from the artistic skill with which it was presented, the values were genuine and genuinely felt. They are not, of course, everybody's values; but they cannot be disposed of by rational argument, they can only be placed in a wider, or less favourable, setting. Equally their force can only be conveyed by the sort of method which Kipling himself adopted. It is easy to forget how unique Kipling's achievement was. Contemporary men of letters like Rider Haggard and Henty may have shared some of his outlook; but they were, of course, less gifted artistically and had less to say. No writer of equal imaginative power has preached more consistently in support of a political ideal.

The kernel of Kipling's political philosophy is his concept of 'The Law'; the kernel of 'The Law', the necessity of obedience. In the *Jungle Books* he says:

. . . *The head and the hoof of the Law and the haunch and the humph is—Obey!*

In *Her Majesty's Servants* a native officer in the Indian Army explains to a Central Asian Chief how obedience, among both beasts and men, is the key to the system's success. Kipling never expounds the law of human society so explicitly as he does the Law of the Jungle, though perhaps one is simply to understand it as a tamer version of the latter. But he continually stresses the

virtue of living in obedience to law of one kind or another. In
The Miracle of Purun Baghat (from the second *Jungle Book*) the
enlightened Prime Minister of an Indian State, turned holy man,
defers to a native Mohammedan policeman, who tells him he is
obstructing the traffic: '. . . He salaamed reverently to the law,
because he knew the value of it, and was seeking for a law of his
own.' In *Letters of Travel* Kipling writes: 'There is an ordained
ritual for the handling of all things, to which if a man will only
conform and keep quiet, he and his will be attended to with the
rest.' In one of his last stories, *The Manner of Men*, Paul says to
Sulinor: 'Serve Caesar. You are not canvas I can cut to advantage
at present. But if you serve Caesar you will be obeying at least
some sort of law.'

What did this mean in practical terms of Empire? Perhaps, for
Kipling, its existence, and the virtue of obeying it, were nine
points of the law. But there is a short, yet pithy, recipe for imperial conduct in *A Song of the English* (1893):

> *Keep ye the law—be swift in all obedience,*
> *Clear the land of evil, drive the road and bridge the ford,*
> *Make ye sure to each his own*
> *That he reap where he have sown,*
> *By the peace among our peoples let men know we serve the*
> *Lord!*

Peace, Order, Justice and Public Works. The same pre-occupations appear in an early comment from New York in *Letters of
Travel:* 'In a heathen land the three things that are supposed to
be the pillars of moderately decent government are regard for
human life, justice criminal and civil, as far as it lies in a man to
do justice, and good roads.' Driving the road and bridging the
ford were always close to Kipling's heart. The story called *The
Bridge-Builders* (*The Day's Work:* 1898) is an example. *Judson and
the Empire* (*Many Inventions:* 1893) expresses contempt for the—
unnamed—Portuguese Empire in East Africa:

'They had built no roads. Their towns were rotting under their
hands; they had no trade worth the freight of a crazy steamer;

and their sovereignty ran almost one musket-shot inland when things were peaceful.'

There were those who were called to rule and those who were called to obey. The rulers themselves, like Aristotelian planets, had to obey their own exacting and predictable code. The moralist/craftsman expected them to live clean and devoted lives, to know their duty and to perform it. Kipling was not interested in bridging the gap between rulers and ruled; but (self-rule apart) the latter had their rights, which the right sort of ruler would naturally respect.

Kipling never seems to have questioned the title of the British to govern India or to have looked forward, with any satisfaction, to their eventual withdrawal. *The Head of the District* (an early story) does not shew much sympathy with the Western-educated Indian senior official. *One View of the Question* (*Many Inventions:* 1893) ridicules, indirectly, the liberal idea that 'upon a day' the white men should depart from India. The day-dream sketched in *His Private Honour* (from the same collection) suggests that Kipling would at that time have preferred an independent, white-settler-governed India, protected by white soldiers with perhaps some Eurasian help: 'a colonized, manufacturing, India with a permanent surplus and her own flag.'[1] His fullest, and perhaps most serious, comment on the possibility of British withdrawal comes from another early story, *On the City Wall:*

'Year by year England sends out fresh drafts for the first fighting-line, which is officially called the Indian Civil Service. These die, or kill themselves by overwork, or are worried to death, or broken in health and hope in order that the land may be protected from death and sickness, famine and war, and may eventually become capable of standing alone. It will never stand alone, but the idea is a pretty one, and men are willing to die for it, and yearly the work of pushing and coaxing and scolding the country into good living goes forward. If an advance be made all credit is given to the native, while the Englishmen stand back and wipe

[1] Cf. Letter No. V in *From Sea to Sea* (1889): 'Imagine an India fit for permanent habitation by our kin, and consider what a place it would be this day, with the painter cut fifty years ago, fifty thousand miles of railways laid down and ten thousand under survey and possibly an annual surplus.'

their foreheads. If a failure occur the Englishmen step forward and take the blame. Overmuch tenderness of this kind has bred a strong belief among many natives that the native is capable of administering the country, and many devout Englishmen believe this also, because the theory is stated in beautiful English, with all the latest political colour.'

Similarly, in *Letters of Travel*, he reports with some sympathy the views of the 'Overseas Club', which 'puts up its collective nose scornfully when it hears of the New and Regenerate Japan sprung to life since the 'seventies.'

Kipling's conviction of the British right to rule in India and elsewhere prompts the question whether he asserted the superiority of British racial stock. Undoubtedly he made some assumption of this kind. 'There must be born a poet who shall give the English *the* song of their own, own, country—which is to say, of about half the world. . . . The Saga of the Anglo-Saxon all round the earth—' he wrote in 1889, when he was twenty-four.[1] In *The Man Who Would Be King* (*Wee Willie Winkie:* 1896) Dan Dravot says of his intended Central Asian subjects: 'I won't make a Nation. . . . I'll make an Empire! These men aren't Niggers; they're English! Look at their eyes—look at their mouths. Look at the way they stand up. They sit on chairs in their own houses. They're the Lost Tribes or something like it and they've grown to be English. . . .' The racial note is sounded in *A Song of the English* (1893) and in the following lines from *The Song of Seven Cities* (*Diversity of Creatures:* 1917):

> *Nor will I rest from search till I have filled anew my Cities*
> *With peoples undefeated of the dark enduring blood.*

It appears, less blatantly, in his comment on Japan in 1889:

'Japan is a great people. Mercifully she has been denied the last touch of firmness in her character which would enable her to play with the whole round world. We possess that— . . . it is our compensation.'[2]

In his address to Winchester College in December, 1915,

[1] *From Sea to Sea* (No. XXXVI).
[2] In another passage in *From Sea to Sea* the Japanese evades Anglo-Indian classification: 'The Chinaman's a native. . . . That's the look on a native's face, but the Jap isn't a native, and he isn't a sahib either.'

Kipling spoke of a world where 'every distinction save one—an aristocracy of blood' had been 'emptied of all significance'. The strange South African story, *The Comprehension of Private Cooper*, appears to have racial degeneracy as its topic.[1]

Nevertheless, Kipling was not a crude or doctrinaire racist. He was not tempted by the will-of-the-wisp of 'unmixed race'. He told the Royal Society of St. George in 1920 that the success of the English had partly been due to their 'immensely mixed origin'. He wanted Boers and English to unite in South Africa as Saxons and Normans had in England (this was de Aquila's vision in *Puck of Pook's Hill*). He was a life-long admirer of the French and of French civilization. He valued Indian spiritual, and Japanese artistic, achievement. His strong men could meet face to face, regardless of racial origin.

In his *Choice of Kipling's Verse* T. S. Eliot distinguishes between two attitudes of Kipling towards India: the softer, affectionate, mood, derived from childhood, which came out in *Kim*, and the harsher, more Anglo-Indian mood of his early manhood. Yet even in his earlier stories Kipling had sympathies reaching beyond British official and military life in India: the attractive story, *Without Benefit of Clergy*, is an example. The law must function intact, but it would not interfere with Indian manners and customs in their proper sphere. Kipling knew more about these than most Englishmen who lived in India in the later nineteenth century. There was much in 'native' India that, like his father[2], he loved and respected; his attitude to the problems of imperial government was a product of this respect, as well as of racial arrogance. At bottom, his vision of Empire did not depend on confidence in the genius, or desire for the glory, of the British race. It depended on a belief in the sanctity of work and discipline.

Where does Kipling fit into the scheme of imperial aims suggested at the beginning of this book? First of all, it is clear that he advocated an idealized form of Imperialism capable of winning,

---

[1] Cf. *Aspects of Kipling's Art* by C. A. Bodelsen (1964).
[2] Lockwood Kipling published a miscellany, called *Man and Beast in India*, in 1891.

in some quarters, moral support. He would, I think, have approved the extension or consolidation of Empire for what I have called the 'Colonizing' or 'Strategic' motives, or for the 'Economic' motive in its higher forms. At least as a young man he was capable of feeling the lust for struggle and excitement that imperial adventures can excite. There is more ebullience in his early work than in most of the utterances of the graver British Imperialists. But his moral sense would hardly have allowed him to approve the 'Aggressive' motive as a ground for serious action, unless reinforced by some other motive. There was no doubt an aggressive element in his response to Rhodes' dream of an Africa painted, as much as possible, red. In *A Song of the English* Capetown is made to say:

> *Hail! Snatched and bartered oft from hand to hand,*
> *I dream my dream, by rock and heath and pine,*
> *Of Empire to the northward. Ay, one land*
> *From Lion's head to Line.*

But Kipling did not only justify the British Empire by the need to maintain or extend British greatness and prosperity. He might not have thought this an ignoble object: it involved hardship and sacrifice as much as a more altruistic ideal. Nevertheless, he held that Duty laid more unselfish commands on the Imperialist. The British Empire (and any other well-run Empire) was a force for the general good. It was for the sake of others that the white man must take up his burden. He was to 'seek another's profit, and work another's gain'.

I have already mentioned briefly what benefits Kipling's white man was to confer. He was, in Vergil's language, to rule the peoples, impose the habit of peace, spare the conquered and 'war down' the proud.[1] He was also, as a number of passages shew, to provide communications and impartial justice and to cope with famines and other disasters. But there is remarkably little said about his duties as a missionary or as an educator.

---

[1] 'Tu regere imperio populos, Romane, memento (Hae tibi erunt artes) pacisque imponere morem, Parcere subjectis et debellare superbos.'—*Aeneid:* Book VI.

Kipling was not perhaps rootedly opposed to British education of subject peoples. The poem *Kitchener's School* shews that he could regard it as an amiable, and even admirable, madness; his *White Man's Burden* included humouring hosts '(ah slowly!) toward the light'. But the little he normally says about it suggests his relative lack of enthusiasm. A visit to the Bengal Legislative Council moved him to write, as a young man of twenty-three: 'Western education is an exotic plant. . . . We brought it out from England exactly as we brought out the ink-bottles and the patterns for the chairs. . . . Now we are choked by the roots of it spreading so thickly in this fat soil of Bengal.' He had not, after all, been to a university himself. He valued local customs and religions. He was interested in discipline rather than social advancement and he preferred the cobbler to stick to his last. His lack of proselytizing zeal appears indirectly in *One View of the Question* where the aristocratic Muslim visitor to London says of the British Liberal Party:

'It is the desire of some of these men—indeed, of almost as many as caused the rotting of the English Army—that our lands and people should accurately resemble those of the English upon this very day. May God, the Contemner of Folly, forbid!'

In *The Man Who Was* (from *Life's Handicap:* 1891) Dirkovitch, the Russian, talks of civilizing Asia and provokes the comment:

'That was unsatisfactory, because Asia is not going to be civilized after the methods of the West. There is too much Asia and she is too old. You cannot reform a lady of many lovers, and Asia has been insatiable in her flirtations aforetime. She will never attend Sunday school or learn to vote save with swords for tickets.'

In 1895 he wrote to the Rev. J. Gillespie:[1]

'It is my fortune to have been born and to a large extent brought up among those whom white men called 'heathen'; and . . . it seems to me cruel that white men . . . should amaze and confound their fellow creatures with a doctrine of salvation imperfectly understood by themselves and a code of ethics foreign to

[1] Quoted in Carrington's biography: p. 361.

the climate and instincts of those races whose most cherished customs they outrage and whose gods they insult.'

Full of admiration for traditional Japanese artistry, he wrote from Kobe in 1889: '. . . we grieved afresh that such a people should have a 'constitution' or should dress every tenth young man in European clothes, put a white iron-clad in Kobe harbour, and send a dozen myopic Lieutenants in baggy uniforms about the streets.'

It is clear from the above that Kipling was neither a 'missionary' in his Imperialist aims nor an advocate of assimilatory methods. Equally he did not favour assimilation in reverse. In spite of *Kim* and of his love for India he held that the white man should remain white. It was right that the white official should know, and respect, the customs of the country; but he must keep the distance appropriate to a ruler. In Kipling's view a real divinity hedged any man with kingly functions; he was to borrow 'the soul that is not man's soul'; he had to become something of a God, in order to lead his fellows. He would approach his work in a mood of dedication and might even be required (cf. *The Knife and the Naked Chalk, The Man Who Would Be King* and, in a different key, *The Brushwood Boy* and *A Deal in Cotton*) to practise sexual chastity. In *The Man Who Would Be King* Peachey Carnahan says to Dan Dravot, whom the local people have taken to be a God: '. . . the Bible says that Kings ain't to waste their strength on women, specially when they've got a new raw Kingdom to work over. . . .' In *A Deal in Cotton* (*Actions and Reactions:* 1909) the mother of the clean-living young administrator—a 'Great One'— is heard at the end of the story symbolically humming the *Magnificat* after her organ practice.

Insofar as Kipling's Imperialism was altruistic—and he certainly valued it as such—it was evidently inspired by the 'Leadership' rather than the 'Missionary' motive. By the same token, he was an advocate of 'exclusive' methods, rather than of assimilation or of its reverse.

In a deeper sense, however, it is questionable how far Kipling's imperial creed really was altruistic. A reading of his works forces, to my mind, the conclusion that he approached the problem of

Empire basically from the point of view of the ruler rather than of the ruled. He never seems to have stopped to ask himself, with a genuinely open mind, what would be best, in the long run, for the peoples under imperial rule. He admired Empire primarily because of the sacrifices and responsibilities it imposed on the rulers, because of the moral qualities it drew forth from them. The rulers were to slave on their subjects' behalf; they were to build them roads and give them justice. But, in the last resort, Kipling's ambitions for the ruling race were not altruistic. It was more important that they should attain grace themselves than that they should confer it. One is reminded of Disraeli's dictum:

'I have endeavoured to develop and strengthen our Empire, believing that combination of achievement and responsibility elevates the character and condition of a people';

or of Lugard's:

'. . . a nation, like an individual, must have some task higher than the pursuit of material gain, if it is to escape the benumbing influence of parochialism and to fulfil its higher destiny.'

Perhaps Kipling's description of himself as a 'political Calvinist'[1] should not be taken too literally. But he certainly seems to have felt the need of an 'elect' in his political philosophy. He was also firmly convinced of the ubiquity of original sin. 'Surely we are only virtuous in compulsion of earning our daily bread,' he wrote, light-heartedly but typically, in 1889. In his story about horses in Vermont (*A Walking Delegate*, from *The Day's Work*: 1898), the yellow horse squeals:

' "Have you no respec' whatever fer the dignity of our common horsehood?" '

and Rod, wise horse, replies:

' "Horse, sonny, is what you start from. We know all about horse here, an' he ain't any hightoned, pure-souled, child of nature. Horse, plain horse, same ez you, is chock-full o' tricks, an' meannesses, an' cussednesses, an' shirkin's, an' monkey-shines, which he's took over from his dam, an' thickened up with his own special fancy in the way o' goin' crooked." '

[1] p. 97 above.

This awareness of original, or at least inherited, sin is a familiar ingredient of Tory political philosophy, with its belief in the need for traditional restraints. Imperialism was Kipling's main political interest; in domestic affairs it is not surprising that he should have been a Tory rather than a Liberal. He had a Tory's distrust of intellectual dogma, together with his straightforward patriotism and his sense of tradition and hierarchy. His Toryism is evident in a number of stories, particularly in *An Habitation Enforced*, from his Sussex period, where the American wife unwittingly discovers her roots in the English countryside. In his Dedication of *The Seven Seas* (1896) to Bombay, the city of his birth, he wrote:

> *And she shall touch and remit*
> *After the use of kings*
> *(Orderly, ancient, fit)*
> *My deep-sea plunderings. . . .'*

'Orderly'; 'ancient'; 'fit': three words at the heart of Tory belief. Two later stories, *A Friend of the Family* and *A Prophet and His Country*, touch on the callowness of youthful civilizations.

In spite of his respect for tradition and for gentle inheritance Kipling came from the middle class himself and so did most of his Indian heroes. At least in later life he was not always impressed by the landed gentry. But he could find in the Tory structure, though weakening, some security for the stability of Empire and for the maintenance of law and discipline against democratic ravages. There was, besides, an affinity between the Tory and the Imperialist faiths. Tories, as Labouchere argued,[1] 'never could believe that people could govern themselves: they always thought it was necessary for some superior class to step in and govern them'.

A rather Carlylesque passage which he wrote in an Indian newspaper article in 1888 shews how Kipling's Toryism and Imperialism went hand in hand: it expresses 'admiration for the Englishmen who live in patriarchal fashion among the People,

---

[1] Thornton: *The Imperial Idea and Its Enemies:* p. 88.

respecting and respected, knowing their ways and their wants; believing (soundest of all beliefs) that "too much progress is bad", and compassing with their heads and hands real concrete and undeniable Things'.

Yet it would be wrong to lay too much stress on the traditional aspects of Kipling's work. There was another side of him that was extremely modern. There was nothing old-fashioned in his interest in engineers and servicemen, in his use of popular language, in the directness of his emotional appeal and in his short-story techniques. No writer of his time was more eager to use and describe new inventions; he realized to the full the power of machines in the modern world; his sense of romance would always respond to fresh mechanical possibilities. Nor has anybody seen more clearly the immense difference that improved communications were bound to make to world affairs. Professor Macmillan records, in *The Road to Self-Rule*, how:

'. . . in Edwardian Oxford many years ago an after-dinner speech of Mr. Rudyard Kipling's offended my youthful optimism, and yet his reiteration of its theme stamped it on my memory: the modern world of mechanized travel he saw as a 'shrinking ball', and it troubled him that its diverse peoples faced the test of living in even closer, almost alarming proximity to one another.'

In this vein Kipling told the Royal Geographical Society, in 1914:

'. . . in a few years, most of our existing methods of transport, together with the physical and mental emotions that accompany them, will be profoundly changed. . . .'

In 1925 he said, at a Chamber of Shipping dinner:

'Everywhere time and space are coming to heel round us to fetch and carry for our behoof, in the wilderness or the market. And that means that it will be possible for us now, as never before, to fuse our Empire together in thought and understanding as closely as in the interchange of men and things.'

Kipling might have foreseen that the effect of improved communications on the Empire could also be a disintegrating one; that they were, in fact, likely to promote Cosmopolitanism rather than Imperialism. Indeed at one period he does seem to have envisaged this. Two stories of his middle period, *With the Night*

Mail (*Actions and Reactions:* 1910) and *As Easy as A.B.C.*
(written in 1912), picture the world under the ultimate governance
of an international body, the Aerial Board of Control. The
earlier story, which revels in technical expertise, is the more
light-hearted. It is set in A.D. 2000. The A.B.C. 'that semi-
elected, semi-nominated body of a few score persons of both
sexes, controls this planet. 'Transportation is Civilization', our
motto runs. Theoretically we do what we please so long as we do
not interfere with the traffic *and all it implies*. Practically, the
A.B.C. confirms or annuls all international arrangements and, to
judge from its last report, finds our tolerant, humorous, lazy little
planet only too ready to shift the whole burden of public administration on its shoulders.' It appears that the A.B.C. was con-
stituted in 1949 and that war, as a paying concern, ceased in
1967. Crete had, till recently, been the last European repository of
autonomous institutions 'and the rest of the archaic lumber
devised in the past for the confusion of human affairs'. But the
Cretans got bored with exploiting the tourist value of their institutions and now they, too, have been taken over. 'The only
people who suffer will be the Board of Control, which is grievously
overworked already.'

Mutatis mutandis the picture recalls, if less poetically, the
visions of an older Victorian who was to become a staunch
Imperialist in his later years. In *Locksley Hall* Tennyson looked
forward not only to 'pilots of the purple twilight, dropping down
with costly bales', but also to:

> . . . *the Parliament of man, the Federation of the world,*
> *There the common sense of most shall hold a fretful realm in*
> *awe,*
> *And the kindly earth shall slumber, lapt in universal law.*

The same dream appeared in his *Ode to Victor Hugo:*

> . . . *England, France, all men to be*
> *Will make one people ere man's race be run:*
> *And I, desiring that diviner day. . . .*

But the predictions of Winwood Reade in *The Martyrdom of*

Man[1] (1872), were perhaps closer to what Kipling had in mind. Reade prophesied an improvement in communications which 'will speedily extinguish national distinctions'. When that happens:

'Governments will be conducted with the quietude and regularity of club committees. The interest which is now felt in politics will be transferred to science. . . .'

As Easy as A.B.C. is a less straightforward story than *With the Night Mail*. It shews the A.B.C., with its personnel picked from different countries, intervening in Northern Illinois, in A.D. 2065, to disperse crowds and forestall riots. The people are mad with anger at a minority called the 'Serviles' who have been agitating for a return to the assemblies, orators and democratic methods of the old days. The danger is summed up by a woman who exclaims: 'Crowds make trouble. They bring back the old days. Hate, fear, blackmail, publicity, 'The People' . . .' In the end the 'Serviles' are taken to London and handed over to an impresario as a kind of music-hall turn.

The world pictured in this story is not altogether attractive. The birth rate has fallen (though there is a hint that the A.B.C. can put this right) and there is a suggestion of people living under nervous strain. One critic[2] sees the story as '. . . a *tour de force* of sustained irony, in which the narrator, a typical product of this Wellsian future in which 'Transport is Civilization', unwittingly reveals the spiritual emptiness of a world which has banished struggle and suffering from life.'

I think this goes too far. I am not sure exactly what view the reader is meant to take of the world in the A.B.C. era, or whether Kipling himself thought of it as a more desirable place than, say, early nineteenth century Europe. Probably not. However, he was not concerned with such comparisons, but to shew *first* what might be the result of improved communications and techniques and *second* what he expected to be the eventual reaction to Democracy—as he conceived it—run riot. On the whole he seems to me to present the A.B.C. as a reasonable solution to the world's increasingly complex problems and to admire the way it goes

[1] Cf. p. 40 above.
[2] W. W. Robson in *Kipling's Mind and Art*.

about its work. What is certain is that he saw a future of this kind as infinitely preferable to the increasing sway of his bugbears, Democracy and Publicity.

I have dwelt on these stories because they shew a more internationally minded Kipling than would seem possible from the bulk of his work. His speech at the 1925 Chamber of Shipping Dinner may suggest that he only explored this path as a brief aberration. But, aberration or not, the stories indicate how easily his Imperialist system, shorn of the glamour of race and tradition, could be adapted to the rule of an international bureaucracy. In the last resort the structure of Kipling's political thought rested on three pillars:

(1) The Law, which no tyranny, whether of the mass or the individual, must be allowed to usurp.

(2) Expert rule by dedicated, hard-working men.

(3) Freedom for the ruled to live their own lives in privacy.

These were the props of the Indian Empire, as Kipling saw it. They were, to his mind, the props of good government everywhere. They are also the props of the A.B.C. *régime*.

In the dedicatory poem at the beginning of *The Five Nations* (1903), Kipling pays tribute to the Imperialists of the future, suggesting that the Imperialist ripples of his day were only the precursors of the grand swell that was to come. His own writings, he felt, had fallen 'weak and wide' of this massive future:

> '*Yet instant to fore-shadowed need*
> *The eternal balance swings;*
> *That wingéd men the fates may breed*
> *So soon as Fate hath wings.*
> *These shall possess*
> *Our littleness,*
> *And in the imperial task (as worthy) lay*
> *Up our lives' all to piece one giant day.*'

Although there were few more wings in store for the British Empire, Kipling seems, in the context, to have been relying on the Five Nations of British settlement to provide the new supermen. At the time of this 'Dedication' it was still possible to have a stirring faith in the Empire; the Boer War had been comforting as well as disquieting. Before Kipling died, however, he must have realized that the reality was unlikely to keep pace with his dream. International politics between the wars may not have encouraged him to revert to the cosmopolitan vein of his Science Fiction stories. Yet the new national imperialisms that were stirring in Europe and the Far East, at the time of his death, proved short-lived; and the conflict with them hastened the dissolution of the old ones. None of them would come near to justifying Kipling's prophecy, unless (which was certainly not what he envisaged) the 'giant day' of Imperialism was to be the moment of independence.

V

The Vision

These are only a few portraits, if perhaps the most notice-
able ones, from the gallery of Late Victorian Imperialism.
The movement attracted adherents from all walks of life.
The more distinguished—politicians, officials, men of action,
journalists, businessmen and writers—formed a kind of Club, or
Companionship, in which the bond of ideas was strengthened by
mutual esteem. Imperialists did not of course necessarily approve
of each other. Chamberlain and Lugard were wary of Rhodes and
Rosebery is said to have found 'the turgid emotionalism of
Kipling' antipathetic.[1] Personal and party differences divided
Chamberlain from Rosebery during the Boer War. But the
devotees of Empire were conscious of dedication to a common
ideal; they often fed, and were warmed by, each other's flames.

The general temper of his writings gives Carlyle some claim to
be regarded as the Grand Old Man of the 'New Imperialism',
though he never dealt with colonial questions in depth. Froude,
who was his friend and disciple as well as biographer, recorded in
Oceana: 'In Carlyle's opinion . . . England's business, if she
understood it, was to gather her colonies close to her and spread
her people where they could breathe again, and send the stream of
life back into her loaded veins.' Kipling admired Carlyle's
writings; W. E. Forster, the first chairman of the Imperial
Federation League, was on intimate terms with him. Ruskin,
another friend of Carlyle, was a very part-time Imperialist; but his
inaugural lecture is supposed to have had a great influence on
Rhodes.

Rosebery and Dilke, though not of the Conservative Party,

[1] *Life of Rosebery* by R. Rhodes James: p. 157.

were drawn to Disraeli as young men. There was a close association between Dilke and Chamberlain at the outset of their political careers. Lugard thought he had helped to convert Chamberlain to an interest in East Africa. Chamberlain was much impressed by Cromer's work in Egypt and paid public tribute to Froude and Seeley. Both he and Rosebery, who made Seeley a K.C.M.G., were deeply influenced by *The Expansion of England*. W. T. Stead, the celebrated journalist, was close to Rhodes and had at one time been associated with Milner. Milner had worked under Cromer in Egypt and much admired him; so did Curzon; Cromer and Curzon both wrote messages of sympathy and congratulation to Milner at the height of the Boer War.

Kipling contributed to the patriotic *National Observer*, edited by W. E. Henley, in the 'nineties. A frequent visitor to South Africa, he knew Rhodes and Milner and was devoted to both. In his works he eulogised Chamberlain ('. . . the idea of our Empire as a community of men of allied race and identical aims . . . we all know the one man who in our time gave present life to that grand conception'); Curzon ('. . . all the qualities that mark a leader of men. . . .'); Rhodes ('Living, he was the land, and dead His soul shall be its soul'); and Milner ('They that dig foundations deep, fit for realms to rise upon. . . .'). Curzon quoted *The White Man's Burden* appreciatively in one of his early Indian speeches.

It is not surprising that a political movement should be interlaced with debts and tributes of this kind, though there was almost something church-like in the depth and piety of Imperialist solidarity. What is perhaps more striking is the extent to which the movement cut across party lines. It is curious how many of the chief Imperialists (Forster, Rosebery, Dilke, Chamberlain, Seeley, Cromer, Milner) had Liberal affiliations at one time or another. How should this be reconciled with the common notion that British Imperialism was a Tory creed, with Disraeli as its prophet?

In theory there seems to be nothing specifically Tory about Imperialism or Imperialist about Toryism. Conservatism is not naturally expansive; Tories, concerned with maintaining domestic traditions, could perfectly well have been 'Little Englanders', in the same sort of way as the Athenian aristocracy was opposed to imperial expansion under Pericles and Cleon. But once expansion had occurred, or where the security or prosperity of the nation seemed to require fresh advance, it was natural that Tory patriotism should rally behind the Empire, so long as the authority of the Crown was upheld and there was no threat to the structure of British life. Tories were less likely than Liberals to be worried by general principles or to feel that the right of self-government was all-important; they were used to providing, or submitting to, leadership at home. Finding an Empire already won, their instinct was to treat it as a permanent possession, while their hierarchical sense tended to prevent them from advocating assimilatory methods.

Equally there was nothing in theory to prevent Whigs and Liberals from embracing the Imperialist cause, so long as they preached a less static, and more proselytizing, brand of Empire. They could pose as the agents of Progress, bringing enlightened views and methods to benighted masses, with the eventual aim of educating these masses, shepherding them towards the light and then leaving them to enjoy self-government. By these standards British rule could be preferred to oriental and African despotism, because it was expected to lead to a greater diffusion of real liberty.[1]

The Radical philosopher and journalist, L. T. Hobhouse, in his book *Democracy and Reaction* (written in 1905) distinguished between the '. . . old Liberal conception of opening to them [the "coloured" races] the road to self-development' and '. . . the new Imperialism', which 'stood not for a widened and ennobled sense of national responsibility, but for a hard assertion of racial supremacy and material force'. Inspired by the 'old Liberal conception', the Whig/Liberal Imperialist could be as active as the Tory in expanding Empire, indeed more so. But, if true to his faith, he would be readier to relinquish control and more of an assimilator in the interval.

Thus Imperialism could find support both in Whig and in Tory (Liberal and Conservative) doctrine; but the two approaches

[1] Cf. p. 40 above.

should not, in theory, have been the same. In practice there *was* some difference of emphasis, as I have suggested in the case of Rosebery;[1] but it was much slighter than might have been expected. In effect Imperialism appeared as a virtually new creed, offering more or less the same attraction to people of both persuasions. It touched a new chord; its converts were not much reached through their existing political sympathies. If it came to be associated primarily with the Conservative Party (in spite of the distinction of many Liberal Imperialists and Liberal Unionists), it was because a confused current of attitudes and events swept the progressive wing of the Liberal Party into anti-Imperialism, rather than because of any fundamental incompatibility between Imperialism and older Liberal thought.

Yet this is not the whole story. The slender differences of approach between Liberal and Tory Imperialists in the late nineteenth century suggest that there must have been some suppression of principle on one side or the other. Either the Tories must have become more anxious to proselytize or the Liberals must have become more authoritarian. The evidence produced in the last two chapters tends to shew that the latter was the case. The stress on 'leadership', the decline in missionary optimism, the receding vision of self-government, were not confined to Tory Imperialists. Whatever their political beliefs, Chamberlain, Cromer and Milner came to use imperial power as paternally as any improving Tory squire. There might be no fundamental incompatibility between Liberalism and Imperialism as such; but there was some real incompatibility between Liberalism and the version of Imperialism normally practised and preached at the turn of the century. There may have been something radical about the new imperial approach, but there was little that was libertarian.

The opinions of Lord Dufferin (1826–1902: Governor-General of Canada 1872–1879 and Viceroy of India 1884–1888) illustrate the move away from genuinely Liberal Imperialism. Dufferin was a moderate Whig who, like Rosebery, combined strong patriotism with a belief that the British race 'has done more than any

[1] p. 70 above.

other to spread abroad the benefits of ordered liberty and constitutional government.' In 1883 he advocated the prudent creation of representative institutions in Egypt. In India he sympathized with 'the legitimate and reasonable aspirations of the
responsible heads of Native society.' But, by the time he left
India, if not before, he was convinced that 'England should never
abdicate her supreme control of public affairs, or delegate to a
minority, or to a class, the duty of providing for the welfare of the
diversified communities over which she rules. . . .'

There is then some justification for regarding Late Victorian
Imperialism as a primarily Tory phenomenon. It comes as no
surprise that Kipling—often, and rightly, regarded as the arche-
type of 'the new Imperialism'—should have been Tory rather
than Liberal in his outlook.

There were many other ways in which Kipling was typical of
the Imperialist movement. The part played by India in his life
could symbolize the central importance of the *Raj* in the whole
imperial scheme. Cromer and Lugard served in India, while
Dilke and Rosebery visited it. Salisbury's ministerial *début* was in
the India Office. Froude described British rule in India as 'an
unexampled success'; Curzon spoke of India as 'the pivot of
empire' and said that, if we lost it, 'I maintain that our sun would
sink to its setting'; Rosebery recalled that, before the Scramble for
Africa, 'our foreign policy was mainly an Indian policy; it was
mainly guided by considerations of what was best for our
Indian Empire. . . .' Even during and after the Scramble the
strategic needs of the *Raj* weighed heavy in the minds of British
statesmen.[1] India was at once the bedrock of British imperial
sway and the least controversial instance of imperial rule. The
foundation of our Indian Empire went back to the buccaneering
days of the eighteenth century. Its continuance largely escaped
serious criticism at home, partly because it was commercially
valuable, partly because it was assumed to confer great benefits
on the Indians, but perhaps mainly because it was an immense
source of pride to the British people. This deep, and not always
articulate, complacency provided a fertile field for fresh im-

[1] Cf. pp. 57–58 above.

perialist seed. In this, as in other respects, India was indeed the pivot of the dependent empire. Later history shewed that the Victorian instinct had been right: India's possession required and supported the possession of other dependencies; its independence led to the independence of the rest.

India, more than any other part of the Empire, recalled the grandeur of Rome. Like other Late Victorian Imperialists Kipling was moved by Rome's imperial example. Cromer compared ancient and modern imperialism; Curzon recalled being invited at Eton 'to contemplate the pomp and majesty, the law and the living influence, of the empire of Rome'. The Roman spirit worked powerfully in Froude and Rhodes; it caused Lugard to describe Britain, in an unusual flight of fancy, as 'the Uganda of the Roman Empire'. Kipling's Roman stories and verses[1] are among his best; by making the Romans British, they made the British feel more Roman. Rome's imperial mission, no matter of controversy but an historical fact, was used to strengthen England's confidence in hers.

I believe that Kipling was also typical of 'the New Imperialism' in his basic indifference to the 'Economic Motive'. Dilke, Froude and Seeley, although more alive to commercial considerations than Kipling, put political and racial factors first. The Proconsuls necessarily valued trade and prosperity; but they seldom behaved as if they represented 'a nation of shopkeepers'. Curzon said in 1898: 'A century ago India in the hands of the East India Company was regarded as a mercantile investment . . . we [now] think much of the welfare of India and but little of its wealth. . . .' Other British Imperialists, like Chamberlain and Rhodes, made considerable use of economic arguments in public; but they seem to have been driven primarily by deeper motives, which they sought to justify by economic advantage. There is no way of proving this; but it can at least be asserted that the Leninist explanation of Imperialism has been pushed too far. Commercial pressure sometimes contributed to imperial advance. Economic arguments served to make the Imperialist ideal hard-headed and

---

[1] *Puck of Pook's Hill, Regulus, The Church at Antioch, Gallio's Song* and the Horatian pastiches in *A Diversity of Creatures* and *Debits and Credits*.

respectable; Rhodes would hardly have proposed philanthropy without five per cent. The economic aims of French and German Imperialism helped to provoke a corresponding British imperial effort, directed towards open markets as well as strategic protection. But it has been shewn convincingly[1] that economic considerations had less effect on official action in the 'eighties and early 'nineties than strategic ones. Even if this were not the case, it seems clear enough that, at bottom, most of the prophets and servants of Late Victorian Empire thrilled to other chords. Their own testimony suggests that a less calculating sense of imperial vocation inspired them.

In his *Rise of our East African Empire* (1893) Lugard advocated the retention of Uganda for commercial, among other, reasons. This was a work aimed at the unconverted public and written with a strictly practical purpose. Even so, the curiously inverted way in which Lugard puts his argument is significant:

'It is well, then, to realize that it is for our *advantage*—and not alone at the dictates of duty—that we have undertaken responsibilities in East Africa.' And again:

'If our advent in Africa introduces civilization, peace and good government, abolishes the slave trade and effects other advantages for Africa, it must not therefore be supposed that this was our sole and only aim in going there. However greatly such objects may weigh with a large and powerful section of the nation, I do not believe that in these days our national policy is based on motives of philanthropy only.'

It is striking that in 1893, after the division of Africa has already taken place, Lugard should feel the need to argue, in a serious book, that a sense of duty was not the *only* motive behind African empire. Nobody, nowadays, would suppose that it could have been. The argument is suggestive of the emotional climate in which Imperialism was bred. Rhodes wrote to Stead in 1891: 'Even a Labouchere who possesses no sentiment should be taught that the labour of England is dependent on the outside world, and that as far as I can see the outside world, if he does not look out, will boycott the results of English labour.' Rhodes believed

---

[1] *Africa and the Victorians.* Cf. pp. 57–59 above.

in this argument but, possessing sentiment, valued others more. One chord to which the Late Victorian Imperialists did, unmistakably, thrill was racial pride. They shared a strong sense of Anglo-Saxon prowess, an inherited conviction that the British were, in one sense or another, a chosen people. Kipling was, again, typical of his fellow Imperialists—though more extreme than some—in the strength of his racial patriotism. The feeling was not a new one. But it gave an impetus to Imperialism because of the growing realization that, in the face of foreign competition, British principles would not expand without power. It was also hardened and confirmed by popularizations of evolutionary theory. If the concept of Evolution appeared to threaten religious belief, it could sometimes become a substitute for it. More than a touch of religious intensity went into the Imperialist ideal: the triumph of Anglo-Saxon unity could be awaited with almost the same fervour as the Second Coming or the Withering Away of the Marxist State. The mystical appeal of Imperialism must, of course, escape, and can easily survive, a detached analysis. It has to be felt to be understood.

Even the more rabid Imperialists (and most of them had some saving sense of humour or reality) did not believe that the British were necessarily more brilliant or attractive than other races. But they felt that they were somehow more *moral:* firmer, less excitable, juster, more humane, more practical and reliable. Benjamin Kidd, in his best-selling *Social Evolution*, suggested that the French were intellectually superior, but that they were too egotistic; it was because of their social cohesion that the Anglo-Saxons were fitter to survive and succeed. '. . . it is qualities such as humanity, strength and uprightness of character, and devotion to the immediate calls of duty without thought of brilliant ends and ideal results, which have largely contributed to render British rule in India successful. . . .' Milner saw British influence in Egypt as 'a force making for the triumph of the simplest ideals of honesty, humanity and justice'. According to Curzon:

'If you look around the world and enquire why it is that in so many foreign countries the Englishman . . . has . . . been invited to undertake, and has successfully undertaken, the task of regeneration and reform, you will find that it has been because of the universal belief in his integrity, his sincerity and his purpose.'

Even Bagehot, an earlier and cooler observer, thought that the English excelled all other nations in the quality of 'animated moderation', in their combination of energy with knowing when to stop: 'There is an infinite deal to be laid against us, and as we are unpopular with most others, and as we are always grumbling at ourselves, there is no want of people to say it. But, after all, in a certain sense, England is a success in the world; her career has had many faults, but still it has been a fine and winning career upon the whole. And this on account of the exact possession of this particular quality.'[1]

Emphasis on the moral virtues of the English both reflected and promoted the creation of 'the public school type', dedicated to integrity, courage and 'the team spirit'. Writing in 1869 Bagehot had noted that 'men are guided by *type*' and that, every so often, 'a new *model* in character is created for the nation'. 'We are most of us earnest with Mr. Gladstone; we were most of us *not* so earnest in the time of Lord Palmerston.' Later in the century Kipling was as influential as anybody in creating a new model for that part of the nation which served the Empire's needs.

The movement to promote Anglo-Saxon unity, or to achieve Imperial Federation, was partly a consequence of this deep concern with race. With the exception of Disraeli, Curzon, Kipling and Cromer, the Imperialists about whom I have been writing started from the viewpoint of the Empire of British settlement. Their interest in the dependent Empire was, in a sense, secondary; if it had not been for India and the 'Scramble for Africa' it might never have developed—except insofar as they aimed to establish fresh settlements of British stock overseas. Even Curzon found an added charm in India because it was 'the continent whence our emigrant stock first came'. Kipling's Imperialism started with India because he was born and afterwards worked there; he later travelled widely in the Empire of British settlement and became deeply interested in the fraternity of British peoples around the globe. Like other British Imperialists he had a love/

---

[1] Bagehot: *Physics and Politics:* chapter 5.

hate relationship (though hate is too strong a word) with the United States. We have seen how Dilke, Froude and Rhodes were pre-occupied with Anglo-American relations.

When it came to the dependent Empire the Late Victorians, as I have already argued, were more 'exclusive' than 'assimilationist'. They approached their work as Leaders, rather than as Missionaries. Something of the older, more Whiggish, spirit of course remained; but the generous urge to spread light, religion and eventual liberty was increasingly overlaid by a more realistic sense of the responsibilities of government. Late Victorian Imperialists sometimes seem to have been possessed by a fit of tidiness on a global scale and to have found a positively aesthetic satisfaction in spreading order. Once more Kipling is found with other Imperialists: with Froude, for instance, who wrote of 'the influence of the English race in their special capacity of leaders and governors of men'; with Lugard, who thought '. . . we have proved ourselves notably capable of dealing with native races. . . .' It was natural that the great Proconsuls should have the same conviction.

The 'Leadership' approach could be distinguished from earlier British attitudes; it could also be contrasted with the general tendency of French imperial theory, which was still assimilationist. The origins of this difference might be traced to earlier periods: the relations of the English with the Scots and Irish could be compared with the success of the French monarchy in gradually imposing political and cultural uniformity on provincial France. Or one could argue that the practical bent of the English, the intellectual bent of the French, turned them into their different courses. However this may be, the difference was striking and its effects are still noticeable.

Already, in the early 'nineties, Lugard had decided that the keynote of our colonial method was 'to rule through and by the natives' and that this made us more popular with them than the German, French, Portuguese and Spanish. 'An arbitrary and despotic rule, which takes no account of native customs, traditions, and prejudices, is not suited to the successful development of an infant civilization, nor, in my view, is it in accordance with the spirit of British colonial rule'.[1] Here is the germ of the theory and practice of "Indirect Rule", which he was later to elaborate, for good and ill, in Nigeria. The notion would have been congenial to Salisbury, who once said of the native races in the House of Lords: 'They will gradually acquire their own proper civilization without any interference on our part.'[2]

The rather static Late Victorian conception of providing 'good government', of keeping native peoples in order without violating their traditions and prejudices, resulted in an obscurity of ultimate aim. There was no settled idea as to how and when the imperial process should end. The reluctance to face such questions was perhaps partly due to the habitual British distaste for distant plans—and partly to the intrinsic difficulty of the problem. What indeed can be the eventual outcome of an idealistic imperial policy that refrains from proselytizing and assimilating—except permanent dominion? The alternative is the eventual abandonment of empire to people who, if the theory is correct, will be as incapable of governing themselves as when they were first subjected to rule. In practice, of course, the dilemma was less acute than this would suggest; whatever the general character of late nineteenth century British imperial rule, it was bound to involve a fair amount of rather haphazard assimilation. The distinction which I have been elaborating cannot have been as clear at the time as it now appears. But there were no doubt some Imperialists who, if they had cared to look ahead, would have accepted the dilemma. Convinced of British superiority, they would have welcomed the continuance of dominion as far into the future as human vicissitudes would allow.

It is significant that increasing vagueness about the future of the dependent Empire was matched by an increasingly precise vision of the future relationship between the settlements of British stock. Where their heart was in it the Late Victorian Imperialists did not shrink from dreams that were hard to realize.

Another obvious weakness in 'Leadership' Imperialism was that, while it in fact offered chiefly material saisfactions to the

[1] Lugard: *Rise of Our East African Empire*, Vol. 2: p. 651.
[2] Kennedy: *Salisbury:* p. 209.

ruled, it appealed to the spiritual values of the rulers; it exalted the national spirit of the latter, while depreciating that of the former. Such discrimination could be justified by a belief in the absolute superiority, whether permanent or temporary, of the ruling race. Many British Imperialists probably did so justify it. They would not regard themselves as a 'master race' entitled to ride roughshod over humanity. But they were convinced of a certain superiority and they believed, with Curzon, that 'the inscrutable decrees of Providence' had laid an imperial mission on their shoulders. Their attitude prompts the doubt which occurs in reading Kipling:[1] Were their imperial motives really as altruistic as they believed them to be? Were they thinking of the best interests of their subjects or of their own virtue? Was there not a refined selfishness, perhaps even a touch of masochism, in their response to the imperial call?[2]

In the Introduction to this book I suggested that Late Victorian Imperialism 'contained elements of withdrawal as well as of expansion'. I had in mind partly the decline in missionary enthusiasm, partly the self-conscious anxiety to consolidate and conserve. The idea of territorial expansion became officially respectable in the 'nineties—yet only after the chief period of actual expansion was over. Kipling's writings sometimes reflect a 'jingo' mood; but much Imperialist preaching shews unexpected restraint. Neither Dilke, Froude nor Seeley clamoured for fresh imperial adventures. Kipling himself laid much more stress on the duty than on the fun of empire.

Even when the mood was expansionist, it was not born of a light-hearted spirit of aggression. One of the decisive arguments in the minds of serious Imperialists was that, if the British Empire lost its cohesion or momentum, it would be outpaced, in the twentieth century, by other Powers. I have quoted a number of instances of this view from Disraeli[3] onwards. It was a view shaped

---

[1] Cf. pp. 107–108 above.
[2] Cf. Curzon's conception of Empire (in a speech at Birmingham in 1907) as a 'pre-ordained dispensation, intended to be a source of strength and discipline to ourselves and of moral and material blessing to others': a mission permeated with 'the sense of sacrifice and the idea of duty.'
[3] Cf. his speech at Aylesbury in 1859: p. 55 above.

by—justifiable—anxiety, not by the crude optimism of nascent power.

It is strange now to find Froude writing in 1888, towards the end of a decade of intense imperial activity:

'I do not believe in the degeneracy of our race . . . but we are just now in a moulting state and are sick while the process is going on.' Seven years later Chamberlain could say:

'We are all prepared to admire the great Englishman of the past . . . but when we come to our own time we seem to lose the confidence which I think becomes such a great nation as ours; and yet, if we look even to such comparatively small matters as the expeditions in which Englishmen have recently been engaged, the administrations which Englishmen have recently controlled, I see no reason to doubt that the British spirit still lives. . . .'

Rhodes wrote to Stead in 1891: 'Your people do not know their greatness; they possess a fifth of the world and do not know that it is slipping from them. . . .'

The Boers seem to have been sustained by a belief in the degeneracy of the British. The desire to disprove decadence was a part of the *fin-de-siècle* mood and had its effect on imperial action. The Late Victorian Imperialists wanted to convince themselves that they were witnessing a beginning and not an end.

Many criticisms can be made—and some have been made here —of the late Victorian attitude towards the dependent Empire. The racial feeling which sustained it may seem distasteful, and at times even ludicrous, today. Yet a feeling of pride and solidarity is necessary to any great communal achievement. The Late Victorians were not only moved by pride of race, but by a sense— however vague and apocalyptic—of serving global ends. Given their opportunities and prejudices, they held to Bagehot's formula and combined remarkable energy with remarkable moderation. Some of their work has lasted and some of it was, plainly, good.

The scheme with which I started suggests the following conclusion: The territorial expansion of the Late Victorian Empire was dictated primarily by the Strategic, secondly by the Economic, thirdly (a bad third) by the Colonizing and Missionary Motives. But these were not the main reasons for which men became Imperialists. The 'Leadership Motive', combined with sophisticated forms of the 'Aggressive Motive', created the spirit in which the agents of Empire set about their work. This particular combination of motives seems to have no parallel in imperial history and points the unique character of the late Victorian Imperialist mood.

VI

The Need

The imperialist motives outlined at the beginning of this book obviously have in common, if nothing else, a tendency to aggrandisement of one kind or another. Empire-building has different moods, but it necessarily involves expansion; and it is supposed to be the nature of the strong and vigorous to expand. Where there are no physical or moral restraints, operating from within or without, the more active will tend to encroach on the more passive. There is nothing new about this maxim, whether regarded as a tautology ('the expansive expand'), or as recording the way powerful people have been found to behave. It has lost none of its validity, though the area of restraint has widened, since ancient times, so as to restrict the forms of, and opportunities for, expansion. Throughout recorded history the abstract injustice of the unprovoked invasion of weaker peoples has been recognized. Throughout recorded history successful conquerors have been resented, either by their victims or by their rivals. But there has also been a certain awareness that, other things being equal, the strong will rule where they can. Thucydides makes his Athenian assert this at Melos as a universal truth, certainly applicable to human conduct and probably to divine. Perhaps it is only in recent times that worldly men have seen anything positively degrading in the role of the conqueror, except when guilty of the worst forms of cruelty or treachery.

The guilt complexes of modern Imperialism developed rapidly, rather in the same way as the sense of guilt at unevenly distributed wealth. These complexes were bound to thrive, because the imperial nations had, for the most part, founded their own political life on liberal and nationalist principles, which reached their heyday in the nineteenth and early twentieth centuries, nearly at the same time as the main Imperialist thrust. It was natural that the imperial peoples should feel a growing embarrassment about preventing their subject races from enjoying principles that were deeply prized at home. More recently, disapproval of Imperialism has widened and hardened into a dogma, partly because former colonies, now independent, heavily outnumber the former Imperialist nations in the *fora* of international argument.

Late nineteenth century Imperialism must have had a longer season, if the Liberal movement had not still been sending ripples round the world. As it was, it only flourished—though with brief intensity—because the Imperialists reacted in four different ways to the apparent conflict between the ideals of Liberty and those of Empire. Either they reconciled their creed with Liberal beliefs, by regarding empire as a preparation for eventual independence, or at least as conveying a more real freedom and enlightenment; or they suppressed their scruples in deference to their view of what the national safety or greatness required; or they decided that the principle of equality did not extend to 'inferior races' and tropic climates; or they largely abandoned the assumptions of liberalism and, with them, a sense of guilt. Imperialists of these two last categories were free to act as earlier Imperialists had done, though usually with more urge to justify as well as to expand and hence with more constructive aims. But in Great Britain these thorough-going Imperialists were never more than a minority in a nation which had traditionally considered itself the home of freedom and still, to a very large extent, attributed its success to liberalism in trade and home politics. So the British Imperialist had to do his work without the firm backing that he coveted. Sometimes a popular wind filled his sails: but it was fickle, and, when it did blow, was apt to blow too hard.

It is strange, or at least ironical, that the disintegration of the imperial system should have occurred at a time when, in most parts of the world (including the newly independent countries), the flame of liberalism has been burning less pure; when, in Europe at least, the idea of nationalism is beginning to carry less weight; when both politics and economics tend everywhere to advance in the direction of larger and more complex organizations.

Nationalism is, of course, far from dead. In many places it is demonstrably alive and kicking. But it is not impossible that reverence for it, as a general principle, will gradually fade—in some places it is already fading—just as reverence has faded, in many parts of the world, for pure liberalism in economic or constitutional processes. It could of course be the case that mankind is being forced into a higher form of civilization (as Hobson, drawing a parallel between societies and individuals, hoped it would[1]) and that, though the present world structure of nation states will survive, the old urge to expand will be increasingly sublimated into acceptable cultural and commercial channels, regulated by international law. But it is also conceivable that, if the force of nationalism declines, there will arise a new order of Imperialists, perhaps no longer operating on an exclusively national basis themselves, who will feel free to attach less weight to the claims of national sovereignty, than to their view of what economic progress or international equilibrium requires.

This is rather remote speculation and perhaps not very profitable. Meanwhile there is no need to labour the distaste with which any encroachment on national independence is generally regarded: 'Imperialism' has become, in most contexts, an ugly word. Many people find it imposssible to look on the agents of Imperialism, whether alive or dead, except in the most unsympathetic light. Yet the men who spent their lives administering imperial possessions were engaged in work which, whether misguided or not, was not degrading. Kipling may have exaggerated; but he was right to see something admirable, even god like, in the qualities of discipline and devotion which, alongside some conventional limitations, the best of them developed. They were men who deserved respect, not contempt; the vulgar sins of metropolitan Jingoism should not be laid on their shoulders.

Nevertheless, unless we are to regard the world, in Fascist terms,

---

[1] J. A. Hobson in his powerful critique: *Imperialism* (1902), Part II: chapter 2–IV.

as created for the benefit of the expansive, we can hardly justify Empire by the ennobling effect of building it.[1] Conquering the world seems a drastic way of finding worth-while work, of reaching self-fulfilment, or of curing a provincial outlook. From the point of view of a global morality empires can only be justified by their benefits to humanity as a whole. Some cases of empire could perhaps be defended on the ground of their contribution to the peace or prosperity of the world, regardless of their local effects. But the impact of an empire on those most directly concerned—its subjects—must usually rank first. There is no need to take the view that political liberty is the supreme good, or that dominion over others is invariably a crime, to believe that, when one people interferes with another, it is committing a wrong, which can only be justified by the expectation of a greater right. As in all human affairs the question seems to be one of balancing gains against losses. There is an initial loss in invading another's rights which can only be compensated by a greater gain. It will not do for this gain to accrue to the invader, unless it appears to be in the best interest of humanity that it should; to do so it must be great enough to counter-balance both the wrong suffered by the invaded and the breach opened by the invasion in customary international morality.

This is an academic approach which will seem to some to be too relative and to leave too much scope to the Imperialist (not necessarily the best judge of his own and his victim's gains or losses). Even by this kind of standard, however, a marginal improvement in the moral excellence of the empire-builder could scarcely be enough to justify imperial expansion. He must be able to shew that his action is important to the general welfare of mankind—and this must usually embrace, except where vital world interests are concerned, the long-term advantage of his subjects. He will normally have to prove the validity, in each case, of the 'Leadership' or 'Missionary' motive and of its corresponding technique.

I have touched earlier on the phenomenon of 'assimilation in reverse'. There is something attractive in the idea of alien rulers

[1] Cf. p. 108 above.

who understand and appreciate their subjects to the point of adopting their manners and beliefs. An approach of this kind has sometimes palliated the harshness of the more selfish types of imperial rule. It can also be associated with the 'Leadership Motive' in cases where the rulers, of tougher stock than their subjects, bring their energy and raw ability to shore up an old civilization. But the more successfully an alien ruler assimilates himself to his subjects, the less noticeable, whether for good or ill, his imperial contribution becomes. Imperialism of this kind ends up by not being Imperialism at all.

The most noticeable contribution is made by the assimilating Imperialist of the 'Missionary' type. He bears a heavy responsibility since, the more thorough and successful he is, the more he causes a kind of cultural genocide. On the other hand he gives of his own and applies the same standards to his subjects as to himself. He starts with an arrogant sense of superiority; but he aims to lessen the distinction between himself and his subjects, not to perpetuate it.

It would be very dogmatic to assert, as a matter of principle, that Imperialism of this sort can never, in any circumstances, be justified from the subject's point of view. Opinions will differ in each particular case; but in theory there seems no reason why such Imperialism should not be beneficial, if the loss to the subject and the pain of his 'conversion' can be shewn to be outweighed by his ultimate gain. In practice this is bound to be an appallingly difficult calculation, which the Imperialist may not be best placed to work out himself. Nevertheless, although we may not have all the elements for judgment, Roman assimilation seems now, by such a yardstick, to have done more good than harm.[1]

There have been few instances, in modern times, of assimilation as complete as in the more civilized parts of the Roman

[1] At least one Englishman felt this in the early days of American colonization. In his *Pilgrims* (1625) Samuel Purchas used the argument to justify a short way with the Indians of Virginia: 'Can a leopard change his spots? Can a savage, remaining a savage, be civil? Were we not ourselves made and not born civil in our progenitors' days? And were not Caesar's Britons as brutish as Virginians? The Roman swords were best teachers of civility to this and other countries near us.'

Empire. In most modern empires it has only been very partially realized, the resources of the imperial power having seldom been applied for a long enough time or on a big enough scale. There are, however, many instances of successfully assimilated individuals, for instance from French-speaking Africa. Among the religions Islam has shewn a remarkable power of assimilation. The comparative ease with which diverse elements have been assimilated into the American way of life suggests that the process need not be an impossibly difficult one, where political resentment or the force of tradition do not erect too much of a barrier.

During the nineteenth century there was a strong tendency to discount the value of 'primitive' art and customs and to assume that 'native' peoples were more barbarous and less well-organized than in fact they were. More recent anthropological study has suggested that, in Africa for instance, tribal traditions were at least preferable to the first, disintegrating, effects of European penetration. The glories and virtues of the African past may have been, understandably, magnified in reaction to the Victorian attitude; but it is difficult to feel certain that the Africans are in the mass better and happier than before their imperial experience. Yet, whatever the failures of European civilization when exported to tropical countries, its material richness and diversity were bound to attract, even without a conscious Imperialist impulse. It was a naturally expansive civilization; once communications had been opened, it was bound to invade less developed regions and to destroy, or corrupt, their culture. Much of value is continually lost, in all parts of the world, as it becomes more closely connected and so more uniform. There are, however, gains as well as losses and most of the losses seem to be inevitable. What developing country, even when proudest of its traditions, has turned its back on Western technology? On the contrary, the ambition of most African and Asian statesmen is (*pace* Gandhi), while preserving what they can of their own values, to create modern civilizations in their countries, replete with the material conveniences of the twentieth century.

British Imperialism was sometimes assimilatory, but more often, as I have already argued, 'exclusive'. Its social techniques tended to be 'exclusive' even when, as in the earlier part of the nineteenth century, it aimed to proselytize. In the latter part of the century the 'Leader' predominated over the 'Missionary'— both in the vision of imperial publicists and as a matter of general fact. Cromer told the Classical Association, a few years before the First World War: 'There has been no thorough fusion, no real assimilation, between the British and their alien subjects, and, so far as we can now predict, the future will in this respect be but a repetition of the past.' The 'Leadership' approach involves less risk of cultural genocide, less danger of destroying the 'soul' of a country and of leaving it at the mercy of cheap, imported, habits and ideas. But it is open to the criticisms suggested in the last chapter; it withholds from subject peoples the full measure of any benefit they can expect to derive from alien rule; it is also likely to fossilize the local institutions that continue under its patronage. What can such an Imperialism hope, in the end, to achieve?

It is difficult to answer this question fairly: just how difficult appears when a particular case, such as that of British rule in India, is considered. The British *raj* conferred a long period of order and peace. Public health was improved; public works constructed; some industries started and a disciplined army created. Law was, within limits, respected; European methods of education were introduced; customs considered unnecessarily cruel were put down. Above all, perhaps, India was united by a common language and a common administrative system. There were considerable achievements. On the other hand the abuse of money-lending flourished; justice was administered fairly, but in an alien manner; generations of educated Indians suffered, or felt themselves to suffer, humiliation. The increasing birthrate seems to have kept pace with increasing prosperity; perhaps there were as many hungry mouths at the end as at the beginning. Were the advantages, from the Indian point of view, on a scale with the genuinely devoted, if not always imaginative, work put in by the British administrators? Kipling makes us respect these administrators; but he cannot shew what would have happened to the country without them. The sum seems as difficult to work out in practice as in theory.

There were, of course, elements of assimilation in British practice in India, as in other parts of the Empire, notably in regard to Higher Education (Macaulay's Minute was one of the starting points) and in later attempts to inculcate parliamentary democracy. But the general conduct of the rulers was such as to emphasize the distinction between themselves and the ruled. The practical benefits of this 'exclusive' type of Imperialism, however real, must be vitiated—except in very simple or self-confident communities—by their coming from an aloof and alien race. Unless a successful division of values and occupations is possible (which it hardly will be for long) the rulers' sense of distinct and perpetual superiority must engender a greater feeling of resentment or inferiority, among their more educated subjects, than is likely to be the case under a genuinely assimilatory system.

In the long run it seems difficult to justify the 'exclusive' type of Imperialism, from the point of view of the subjects, except during a period of preparation or recovery. When applied for some definite purpose or for a limited period of time, it may have real value, so long as it does not engender too deep and too sterile a sense of inferiority. It may form a useful bridge between two types of civilization, a way of introducing modern techniques with the minimum of tears. Few developing countries can be expected to shew Japan's energy and talent in borrowing independently from other cultures. The process of economic modernization calls for greater administrative resources than most backward countries, starting from near scratch, can hope to muster. One modern African Head of State is said to have regretted that his country never passed through an imperial apprenticeship. As a transitional expedient 'exclusive' Imperialism has the advantage over assimilation of leaving the culture of the subject country more native and intact.

Stripped as far as possible of the element of racial domination, and regarded as a temporary phase, the 'exclusive leader' type of Imperialism approaches the trusteeship system for colonies advocated earlier this century by opponents of jingo Imperialism. Hobson laid down that 'all interference on the part of civilized white nations with 'lower races' is not prima facie illegitimate', provided the aim of the interfering nation was disinterested and progressive and its activities suitably organized for the general good. Lord Attlee[1], in 1937, expressed a Socialist hope:

'In time there might develop an international civil service over all the world, drawn from the nationals of many countries but inspired by a common ideal: the raising of the standard of life and culture of the less advanced races. . . .'

Such a service has, of course, since come into being, on a limited scale, under the aegis of the United Nations. It has not so far usurped, or attempted to usurp, the prerogatives of imperial power, except when required to do so in peacekeeping operations of limited scope. But such operations might, in time, become more extensive; so might the role played by United Nations experts in economic development.

As we have seen, even Kipling toyed with the idea of an international civil service, though not specifically in connection with the less advanced races. He also foresaw, in his Science Fiction stories[2], a decrease in traditional political activities. Here again it is conceivable that, as civilization becomes still more complex and technical and as communications knit the world still more closely together, political opinions everywhere will get less individualist and self-assertive. People in the 'advanced' parts of the world may gradually feel less pride about their own share in public administration; they may become readier to submit to the rule of 'professionals', so that they can keep their interest and energy for their private work and lives. Perhaps it is not too fantastic to discern already a few indications of a tendency in this direction in people's attitude to politics in the European countries. If such a tendency should grow, it could in due course spread to the developing world, which might come to care less about the origin of its administrators, so long as they appeared in the guise of dedicated technicians rather than as a privileged class—and shewed themselves able to create prosperity. It would be rash to overrate this possibility and perhaps wrong to desire it; but the prejudices of future generations will not necessarily be the same as ours.

[1] Quoted in *Concept of Empire*.   [2] pp. 110–113 above.

One of the most striking after-effects of the Imperialist scramble has been the growth of feelings of responsibility in the developed countries for the economic welfare of the former colonies. At the turn of the century the European opponents of Empire were not much exercised by such feelings. As a rule they seem to have been moved less by care for the fox than by disgust with the foxhunter. Hobson, thinking primarily of the metropolitan countries themselves and of their internal and external conflicts, argued against the baneful effects of overseas investment. If the 'haves' now feel a sense of economic obligation towards the 'have-nots', it is largely Imperialism's doing. As a result, the private investment of the imperial era has come to be supplemented by aid programmes which, however inadequate to the immense demand, would have been inconceivable a century ago.

Philanthropy, sharpened by some sense of remorse, urges aid towards the developing countries. The remorse carries echoes, though so far muted ones, of the social conscience that afflicted some of the rich before the last war. At the same time it is being argued that the economic self-interest of the richer countries demands the economic development of the poorer, just as their political self-interest requires peace and stability in the developing world.[1] Foreigners working or living in 'developing' countries may sometimes be tempted to regard them as being as far off from the 'economic take-off' as they seemed to late nineteenth century Imperialists to be from political independence. But perhaps the better endowed are not too remote from this 'take-off', if only substantial aid could be effectively and continuously applied, until local skills can be developed and they can find their economic, as well as political, feet.

The difficulties are formidable and can easily be under-stressed in argument. Yet men on the spot, like Kipling's old Japan hands,[2] may be misled by the natural cynicism of the experienced and by the reluctance of watched pots to boil. It is much too early to judge what future lies in store for most of the developing coun-

[1] Cf. *The Rich and the Poor Nations* by Barbara Ward.
[2] Cf. p. 103 above.

tries. There is scarcely any real precedent. It would be as wrong to prophesy failure as to assume automatic success.

It is however fair to recognize that the provision of effective aid, where there is no direct power to administer, can pose real problems.[1] Independence has come suddenly to a number of countries—not in all cases in answer to the kind of urge that has lifted countries to power and prosperity, by their own efforts, in the past. The developing countries have not yet had time to shew how far they will all be able to evolve, from their own resources, effective forms of the complex modern civilization which confronts them.

There is no way back to the pre-imperial past. Three possibilities seem to remain:

(a) The developing countries will eventually achieve success, and emerge as developed countries, by maintaining stability, using their own energies and employing, without being dominated by, foreign aid.

(b) They (or some of them) will fail to develop fully and will remain, in the mass, near the subsistence level. Meanwhile discouraged *élites* will rule, more or less insecurely, in the capitals. There will be a tendency to devote foreign aid to prestige projects and to hold foreign scapegoats responsible for the failure of the millennium to arrive.

(c) The less viable of the developing countries will come under some new form of imperialism which, as suggested tentatively earlier in this chapter, could be less narrowly national or racial in tone. It could be based on colour or on a continental grouping or on an international social or religious creed. Or it could be 'neo-colonialist' in tone—a determined, though perhaps partly concealed, effort of administration, undertaken by the business interests of the developed world, with some local cooperation, as the

---

[1] This was Milner's experience in Egypt in the 'nineties: 'European skill is useless without European authority. Wherever you turn, that cardinal fact stares you in the face.'

only apparent way of maintaining their markets or sources of supply. Or, under the aegis of the United Nations or of some other international organization, it could take on a more disinterested character and realize the notion of trusteeship more completely than has yet been the case.

Of these three possibilities the second (*b*), if perpetuated, would presumably be the worst. It might be held to justify the Imperialist as proving the discredited slogan that 'these people cannot govern themselves', or as suggesting that they should have had a longer period of apprenticeship to modern civilization under imperial rule. Yet, if this were to be the ultimate fate of all or most of the developing countries, it would stand as a heavy indictment of the interference of the richer and more powerful nations in their way of life. The expansive urge that took European missionaries, merchants, soldiers and administrators to the tropical countries would have ended in destruction and failure.

The first possibility is the one that, for long to come, the world will assume and try to promote. Its achievement depends on men who mostly are, or have been, bitterly hostile to Imperialism. But their success could suggest that the more effective Imperialists, by whatever motives inspired, sowed good seed as well as bad; that the experience of empire stimulated, as well as destroyed.

The third possibility covers a multitude of sins and virtues. Certain forms of 'neo-imperialism', based on economic manipulation or on fanaticism of colour or belief, would confirm that the imperialist urge is deeply or widely rooted, but would also suggest the ultimate failure of earlier Empire-building. On the other hand any strengthening of international administration in the more backward countries would (if it ever became acceptable) presumably escape the stigma of 'Imperialism', yet profit from—and in some measure vindicate—its achievements.

The great moral weakness of most imperial attitudes has been to insist on a double standard: national pride for the rulers, but not for the ruled. The standard must somehow become single before empire—in the sense of government effectively carried on by aliens—ceases to pose moral problems. This could come about, in theory, either through complete assimilation or through complete assimilation in reverse. Otherwise it must depend on the abandonment by both sides of purely national aims.

Perhaps, in the last resort, the main achievement of the great Empires was to serve the necessary, if partly regrettable, purpose of bringing the world closely together. Disaster, in the shape of war or famine, may intervene; we may prove incapable of extending, or even maintaining, the complex machinery of our civilization. But, short of disaster, modern techniques and communications seem in time likely to bring about, over much of the globe, a world civilization comparable in its universality (though not necessarily in its centralized direction) to the Mediterranean civilization of Rome. Imperialism, which appeared in the nineteenth century as the supreme manifestation of national feeling, could yet be remembered as the most effective cosmopolitan force.

List of Principal Works Consulted

BAGEHOT, Walter: *Physics and Politics* (1869).

BENNETT, G. (editor): *The Concept of Empire, Burke to Attlee 1774–1947* (1953).

BODELSEN, C. A.: *Studies in mid-nineteenth century Imperialism* (1923).

BROWN, Hilton: *Rudyard Kipling: A new appreciation* (1945).

BUCKLE, G. E. (Moneypenny and Buckle): *Life of Disraeli* (two-volume edition: 1929).

CALLANDER, T: *The Athenian Empire and the British* (1961).

CAMBRIDGE HISTORY OF THE BRITISH EMPIRE:
Vol. II *The New Empire 1783–1870*,
Vol. III *The Empire-Commonwealth 1870–1919* (1959).

CARRINGTON, C. E.: *The British Overseas* (1950).
Rudyard Kipling: His life and work (1955).

CHAMBERLAIN, Joseph: *Mr. Chamberlain's Speeches* (edited by Charles Boyd: 1914).

CROMER, Lord: *Modern Egypt* (1907; new one-volume edition: 1911).
'Ancient and Modern Imperialism' (an address to the Classical Association: 1910).

CURZON, Lord: *Speeches by Lord Curzon of Kedleston, Viceroy and Governor-General of India* (four volumes: 1900, 1902, 1905 and 1906).

DAVIDSON, John: *The Testament of an Empire Builder* (1902).

DESCHAMPS, H.: *The French Union* (1956).

DICTIONARY OF NATIONAL BIOGRAPHY

DILKE, Sir Charles, Bt.: *Greater Britain: A Record of travel in English-speaking Countries during 1866 and 1867* (fourth edition of 1869).
Problems of Greater Britain (1890).

LIST OF PRINCIPAL WORKS CONSULTED

DUNN, W. H.: *James Anthony Froude. A biography 1857–1894* (1963).

ELIOT, T. S.: *A Choice of Kipling's Verse* (1941).

FROUDE, J. A.: 'England and her Colonies' (originally published in *Fraser's Magazine*, January 1870), and
'The Colonies Once More' (August 1870). (Both these essays were reprinted in *Short Studies on Great Subjects:* new edition of 1893).
Oceana: or England and her Colonies (1886).
The English in the West Indies (1888)

GARVIN AND AMERY: *Life of Joseph Chamberlain* (four volumes: 1932–1951).

HALLETT, R.: 'The European Approach to the Interior of Africa in the Eighteenth Century' (article in the *Journal of African History:* 1963).

HALPERIN, V.: *Lord Milner and the Empire* (1952).

HANCOCK, W. K.: *Argument of Empire* (1943).

HARGREAVES, John D.: *Prelude to the Partition of West Africa* (1963).

HOBHOUSE, L. T.: *Democracy and Reaction* (1905).

HOBSON, J. A.: *Imperialism* (1902).

JENKINS, R.: *Sir Charles Dilke: A Victorian Tragedy* (1958).

KENNEDY, A. L.: *Salisbury 1830–1903: Portrait of a Statesman* (1953).

KIDD, Benjamin: *Social Evolution* (1894).

KINCAID, D.: *British Social Life in India 1608–1937* (1938).

KIPLING, Rudyard: Published prose and verse, including:
Something of Myself (1937).
A Book of Words (selections from speeches and addresses delivered between 1906 and 1927: 1928).

LEROY-BEAULIEU, P.: *De la Colonisation chez les Peuples Modernes* (1874).

LOCKHART AND WOODHOUSE: *Rhodes* (1963).

LUGARD, Captain (later Lord): *The Rise of Our East African Empire: Early Efforts in Nyasaland and Uganda* (1893).

LYALL, Sir A.: *The Life of the Marquis of Dufferin and Ava* (1905).

LIST OF PRINCIPAL WORKS CONSULTED

MACMILLAN, W. M.: *The Road to Self-Rule: A Study in Colonial Evolution* (1959).

MELLOR, G. R.: *British Imperial Trusteeship: 1783–1850* (1951).

MILNER, Lord: *England in Egypt* (1892).
The Nation and the Empire (speeches, published with an Introduction: 1913).

MOON, P. T.: *Imperialism and World Politics* (1926).

PERHAM, Margery: *Lugard: The Years of Adventure* (1956).
Lugard: The Years of Authority (1960).

PISANI-FERRY, F.: *Jules Ferry et le Partage du Monde* (1962).

POPE-HENNESSY, James: *Verandah: Some Episodes in the Crown Colonies 1867–1889* (1964).

READE, Winwood: *The Martyrdom of Man* (1872; seventeenth edition, 1903).

RHODES JAMES, R.: *Rosebery* (1963).

ROBERTS, S. H.: *The History of French Colonial Policy 1870–1925* (1928).

ROBINSON, R., with J. GALLAGHER and A. DENNY:
Africa and the Victorians: The Official Mind of Imperialism (1961).

ROSEBERY, Lord: *Lord Rosebery's Speeches 1874–1896* (published by Neville Beeman).

RUTHERFORD, Andrew (editor): *Kipling's Mind and Art* (essays by various authors: 1964).

SEELEY, Sir J. R.: *The Expansion of England. Two Courses of Lectures* (1883).

SHANKS, Edward: *Rudyard Kipling: A study in literature and political ideas* (1940).

SMITH, Adam: *Wealth of Nations* (Book IV: Chapter 7) (1776).

SMITH, V.: *The Oxford History of India* (second edition: 1923).

STEAD, W. T.: *The Last Will and Testament of Cecil John Rhodes* (1902).

STERN, J.: *The French Colonies, Past and Future* (1944).

STRAUSS, W.: *Joseph Chamberlain and the Theory of Imperialism* (1942).

TACITUS,: *Agricola, Germania* and *Histories*.

TENNYSON, Lord: *Poems*.

LIST OF PRINCIPAL WORKS CONSULTED

THORNTON. A. P.: *The Imperial Idea and its Enemies* (1959).
THUCYDIDES: *History of the Peloponnesian War*.
TREVELYAN, G. O.: *Life and Letters of Lord Macaulay* (1878).
WILLIAMS, B.: *Cecil Rhodes* (1921).
ZETLAND, Lord: *Lord Cromer* (1932).

Index

INDEX

INDEX

India, the Indian Empire, the Indians, 11, 18, 19, 21, 24, 25, 27, 30, 35, 36, 37, 41, 43, 45, 46, 47, 48, 57, 58, 59, 61, 66, 68, 74, 76, 79, 81, 83–5, 86, 87, 88, 92, 93, 94, 95, 96, 98, 99, 100, 102, 103, 104, 107, 109, 113, 119, 120, 122, 123, 135, 136
Indian Mutiny, 42, 61
Ionian Islands, 43
Ireland, the Irish, 41, 75, 87, 92
Islam, 18, 106, 134
Italy, the Italians, 80

James I, 35
Japan, the Japanese, 11, 71, 87, 99, 103, 104, 107, 136, 138
Jews, the, 24, 55

Kenya, 59
Khartoum, 66
Kidd, Benjamin, 59, 122
Kimberley, John, first Earl of, 49
Kipling, Lockwood, 104
Kipling, Rudyard, 13, 14, 26, 67, 81, 89, 95–114, 115, 119, 120, 122, 123, 124, 126, 131, 135, 137, 138
Kobe, 107

Labouchere, Henry, later Lord Taunton, 109, 121
Labuan, 41, 49
Lawrence, T. E., 34
Leninist, 120
Leroy-Beaulieu, Paul, 29, 30, 89
Liverpool, 38
Liverpool, Robert, second Earl of, 37
Livingstone, David, 37
London Company, 35
Louisiana, 27
Lugard, Captain F. J., later Lord, 59, 108, 115, 116, 119, 120, 121, 124
Lyautey, Maréchal, 33, 34

Macaulay, Lord, 19, 43, 46, 47, 48, 49, 80, 84, 136
Macdonald, Rev. F. W., 97
Macmillan, Professor W. M., 48, 110
Macpherson, Sir John, 36
Madagascar, 27, 32
Madras, 47, 80
Majuba, 66
Malaya, 11, 35, 53, 71
Mansfield, William, first Earl of, 45
Marxist, 122
Mauritius, 37, 50
Melos (*Melian Dialogue*), 21, 129
Mill, James, 45
Mill, John Stuart, 29, 86
Milner, Alfred, Viscount, 59, 62, 78, 79, 81–3, 96, 99, 116, 118, 122, 139
Moon, P. T., 57
Morocco, the Moors, 18, 33, 40
Munro, Sir T., 43, 47

Napoleon I, 27, 36, 45, 63
Napoleon III, 33
Nash, John, 46
New Caledonia, 27
New England, 34
New Guinea, 56
New York, 101
New Zealand, 35, 37
Niger, Nigeria, 37, 56, 57, 72, 125
North Borneo, 56
Nova Scotia, 35
Nyasaland, 56, 57

Palmerston, Henry, third Viscount, 35, 40, 42, 63, 74, 89, 123
Pennsylvania, 34
Pericles, 20, 21, 117
Persia (Iran), 19, 20, 83
Peru, 87
Platonic, 98
Polynesia, 86
Pope-Hennessy, Sir John, 49
Portugal, the Portuguese, 18, 32, 101, 124

INDEX